Magento
Beginner's Guide

Create a dynamic, fully featured, online store with
the most powerful open source e-commerce software

William Rice

BIRMINGHAM - MUMBAI

Magento
Beginner's Guide

First published: March 2009

Production Reference: 1200309

Published by Packt Publishing Ltd.
32 Lincoln Road
Olton
Birmingham, B27 6PA, UK.

ISBN 978-1-847195-94-4

www.packtpub.com

Cover Image by Parag Kadam (paragvkadam@gmail.com)

Credits

Author

William Rice

Reviewer

Jose Argudo Blanco

Acquisition Editor

David Barnes

Development Editor

Swapna V. Verlekar

Technical Editor

Amey Kanse

Copy Editor

Sneha Kulkarni

Indexer

Hemangini Bari

Production Editorial Manager

Abhijeet Deobhakta

Editorial Team Leader

Akshara Aware

Project Team Leader

Lata Basantani

Project Coordinator

Rajashree Hamine

Proofreaders

Jeff Orloff

Chris Smith

Production Coordinators

Rajni R. Thorat

Dolly Dasilva

Cover Work

Rajni R. Thorat

About the author

William Rice is a software training professional who lives, works, and plays in New York City. He is the author of two books on Moodle—*Moodle E-Learning Course Development* and *Moodle Teaching Techniques*. His indoor hobbies include writing books and spending way too much time reading sites such as Slashdot and www.ted.org. His outdoor hobbies include orienteering, edible wild plants, and practicing archery within sight of JFK Airport. William is fascinated by the relationship between technology and society: how we create our tools, and how our tools in turn shape us. He is married to an incredible woman who encourages his writing pursuits, and has two amazing sons.

About the reviewer

Jose Argudo is a web developer from Valencia, Spain. After finishing his studies he started working for a software company. He always works with PHP, a language he learned to love. Now, after six years, he is confident in his experience and has started to work as a freelance, in an attempt to give his personal vision to the projects he undertakes.

Working with Joomla!, CodeIgniter, CakePHP, jQuery, and other well-known open source technologies and frameworks, he expects to build stable and reliable applications that reflect his own vision of the Web.

To Silvia and my family

Dedicated to my wife, whose patience and support make my writing career possible.

Table of Contents

Preface

Magento is the world's most evolved e-commerce solution. It runs on the Apache/MySQL/ PHP platform. From a single installation you can control multiple storefronts, all of which share the customer and product information. Magento's templates and themes enable you to customize the look and feel of your store, even optimizing it for mobile phones. Magento's extensions enable you to connect it to a large number of payment gateways and shipping services. Modular code enables you to upgrade your Magento installation while retaining your customizations. Support is provided free of cost by an active open source community, and also by subscription to Varien—the company behind Magento.

This book provides guidance in the form of a step-by-step approach to building a simple, effective online store. The book covers the key features of Magento that will help you get your store up and running. It guides you through installation, configuration, populating your store with products, accepting payments, maintaining relationships with your customers, and fulfilling orders.

When you create an online store with Magento, you usually follow a defined series of steps. This book is arranged to support that process. Each chapter shows you how to get the most from one step.

You will learn to customize the default Magento storefront, so that it becomes your store. You will also learn about Magento's directory structure, and where some of the elements of a store are customized. This experience will help you if you decide to go beyond this book and install new themes, or create your own themes.

As you work your way through each chapter, your store will grow in scope and sophistication. By the time you finish this book you should have a basic, but complete, working online store.

What this book covers

Chapter 1 focuses on what you can do with Magento and a walk-through of a store using the features we will cover.

Chapter 2 covers the installation of Magento on a low-cost hosting service.

Chapter 3 focuses on creating categories and attributes, a necessary step before you can build your catalog of products.

Chapter 4 focuses on the configuration of tax rates and rules to automatically apply the correct sales tax based upon the type of product and the purchaser's location.

Chapter 5 focuses on adding products to your store with detailed descriptions, images, and inventory information.

Chapter 6 focuses on the customization of the default storefront to make it your own.

Chapter 7 focuses on presenting related products to your shoppers, offering products for sale in sets, and giving your customers options such as size, color, manufacturer, and more.

Chapter 8 focuses on managing customer accounts and configuring store contact options.

Chapter 9 focuses on configuring Magento's default payment options such as PayPal, credit cards, check/money order, and purchase orders.

Chapter 10 focuses on offering customers a variety of shipping options, connecting to shippers such as UPS, FedEx, and USPS, and creating customized shipping rates.

Chapter 11 covers the walk-through of fulfilling an order and discovering options for handling order fulfillment, by observing the lifecycle of an order in Magento.

Appendix A has step-by-step directions in one place, and eliminates the explanations and so that you get just the steps you need.

Who this book is for

This book is for anyone who wants to create an online store using Magento. If you are a non-technical person and are discouraged by the complexity of this powerful e-commerce application, this book is ideal for you.

Conventions

In this book, you will find a number of styles of text that distinguishs between different kinds of information. Here are some examples of these styles, and an explanation of their meaning.

Code words in text are shown as follows: "You can see your server's PHP information by uploading and displaying a web page that has the `phpinfo` function."

A block of code will be set as follows:

```php
<?php
phpinfo();
?>
```

New terms and **important words** are shown in bold. Words that you see on the screen, in menus or dialog boxes for example, appear in our text like this: "clicking the **Next** button moves you to the next screen".

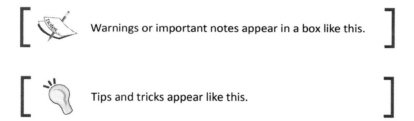

Warnings or important notes appear in a box like this.

Tips and tricks appear like this.

Reader feedback

Feedback from our readers is always welcome. Let us know what you think about this book—what you liked or may have disliked. Reader feedback is important for us to develop titles that you really get the most out of.

To send us general feedback, simply drop an email to feedback@packtpub.com, and mention the book title in the subject of your message.

If there is a book that you need and would like to see us publish, please send us a note via the **SUGGEST A TITLE** form on www.packtpub.com, or send an email to suggest@packtpub.com.

If there is a topic that you have expertise in and you are interested in either writing or contributing to a book on, see our author guide on www.packtpub.com/authors.

Customer support

Now that you are the proud owner of a Packt book, we have a number of things to help you to get the most from your purchase.

Errata

Although we have taken every care to ensure the accuracy of our contents, mistakes do happen. If you find a mistake in one of our books—maybe a mistake in text or code—we would be grateful if you would report this to us. By doing so, you can save other readers from frustration, and help us to improve subsequent versions of this book. If you find any errata, please report them by visiting http://www.packtpub.com/support, selecting your book, clicking on the **let us know** link, and entering the details of your errata. Once your errata are verified, your submission will be accepted and the errata added to any list of existing errata. Any existing errata can be viewed by selecting your title from http://www.packtpub.com/support.

Piracy

Piracy of copyright material on the Internet is an ongoing problem across all media. At Packt, we take the protection of our copyright and licenses very seriously. If you come across any illegal copies of our works in any form on the Internet, please provide us with the location address or website name immediately, so that we can pursue a remedy.

Please contact us at copyright@packtpub.com with a link to the suspected pirated material.

We appreciate your help in protecting our authors, and our ability to bring you valuable content.

Questions

You can contact us at questions@packtpub.com if you are having a problem with any aspect of this book, and we will do our best to address it.

1
Introduction

Magento is an open source e-commerce system that runs on most web-hosting services. It is one of the most powerful, flexible, and customizable e-commerce systems at your disposal. It is also the fastest-growing e-commerce system available on the market.

Magento offers you an extensive suite of powerful tools for creating and managing an online store. As your online store grows, you can be sure that this robust e-commerce system will handle your needs. However, getting started with Magento can be difficult without the right guidance. This book provides that guidance in the form of a step-by-step approach to build a simple and effective online store. As you follow along with the guided lessons, you will see how an online coffee store is created from the ground up. This book will do more than just show you what you need to do when you build your store. We will discuss why we choose certain options and how to make the best decisions when faced with Magento's many options.

This step-by-step beginner's guide takes the pain out of using the world's best open source e-commerce solution. It guides you through installing the software, configuring your store, populating your store with products, accepting payments, maintaining relationships with your customers, and fulfilling orders.

The scope of this book

This book is a step-by-step guide to getting a basic store up and running as quickly as possible. We will use a fraction of Magento's features. However, we will cover all of the features that you need to roll out your store. By the time you finish this book, you will have a store that presents products singly and in groups, makes products easy to find, suggests related products, accepts a variety of payments, informs customers of the status of their orders, and more.

Beyond this book

Magento enables you to create several stores that you can control from the same administrative interface. For example, you could have a discount store, a retail store, and a wholesale store—all controlled from the same Magento installation. To make the administration even easier, these stores can share payment and customer information. Although multiple storefronts are beyond the scope of this book, what you learn about setting up a single store will be applicable to any storefronts that you decide to add later.

Although Magento enables you to accept payment in multiple currencies, this book shows you how to create a store that accepts a single currency. However, the payment methods that you set up for the single currency can also be used for multiple currencies if you decide to expand your store in that direction.

This book shows you how to sell products in groups and how to display related products when a shopper is looking at a product. Magento also offers you the ability to create up-sells for your products. The procedures that you will learn to create related products are very similar to the procedures required to create up-sells.

The look and feel of your storefront can be customized in detail. You can customize the layout, color scheme, icons, graphic elements, and text of your storefront. You can display featured products on any page. You can install entirely new themes to change the look and feel of your store for a season, or whenever you want.

In this book you will learn how to customize the default Magento storefront just enough so that it becomes your store. You will learn about Magento's directory structure and where some of the elements of a store are customized. This experience will help you if you decide to go beyond this book and install new themes, or create your own themes.

Time for action: Tour the demo store

Before we start creating our demonstration store, let's take a tour of how the store will look like. We will look at some of the features that we will learn to use in this book.

   1. The front page of our demo store has been slightly customized from the default Magento installation. We changed it a bit to get rid of the standard Magento appearance.

Notice the logo in the upper left corner. We will learn how to customize this in Chapter 6. We will also learn how to customize the welcome message in the upper right corner, the content of the main area of this page, and the callout in the right column.

The links in the upper right corner (**My Account, My Wishlist**...**Log In**) are standard Magento features. We will leave them as they are in our installation.

You can see product categories across the top of the page (**Blended, Single Origin**... **Coffee Accessories**). We will learn how to put products into categories and subcategories, making them easier for your shoppers to find.

2. Now, let's look at one of these category pages:

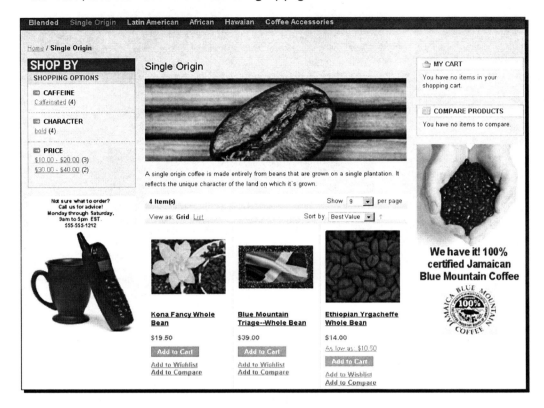

The callout from the front page is displayed in the right column again. There is also a customized callout in the left column: **Not sure what to order?**

Notice that the customer can now filter the products in this category by several options: **Caffeine, Character**, and **Price**. These are called **Attributes**. You will learn how to create custom Attributes for your products. You will then learn how to make your custom and Magento's built-in Attributes show up in the navigation menu.

3. Let's look at the page for an individual product:

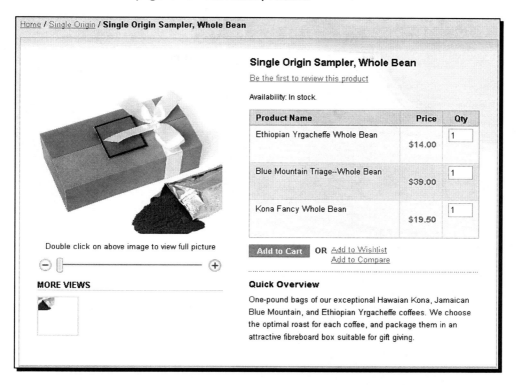

Home / Single Origin / **Single Origin Sampler, Whole Bean**

Single Origin Sampler, Whole Bean

Be the first to review this product

Availability: In stock.

Product Name	Price	Qty
Ethiopian Yrgacheffe Whole Bean	$14.00	1
Blue Mountain Triage--Whole Bean	$39.00	1
Kona Fancy Whole Bean	$19.50	1

Double click on above image to view full picture

Add to Cart OR Add to Wishlist
Add to Compare

MORE VIEWS

Quick Overview

One-pound bags of our exceptional Hawaian Kona, Jamaican Blue Mountain, and Ethiopian Yrgacheffe coffees. We choose the optimal roast for each coffee, and package them in an attractive fibreboard box suitable for gift giving.

This product is actually a group of products presented together on the same page. When the customer clicks on the **Add to Cart** button, all three products in this group get added to the Shopping Cart at once. This is an example of a **Grouped Product**. This is useful for items that are usually sold as sets, such as a suit (jacket plus pants) or a dining room set (table plus chairs).

4. Let's look at the checkout process next:

Notice that the checkout page is divided into five tabs: **Billing Information** through **Order Review**. All of these tabs are on the same page. This makes it easy for the customer to navigate from one part of the checkout process to the other. Also, notice the **Checkout Progress** in the right column. The customer always knows exactly where (s)he is in the checkout process. This is Magento's one-page checkout, and it is a standard feature.

In the previous screenshot, you can see that we are offering the customer a choice of shipping options. The top-two options use **United Parcel Service**. You will learn how to make Magento interface with shipping providers, so that it can look up the charges for various types of shipping from those providers. The third option doesn't state a specific shipper. However, it does state that shipping charges are based on the order total. You will also learn how to create shipping tables that calculate shipping charges based on an order's destination, weight, and total.

5. Now, let's look at the payment part of the checkout page:

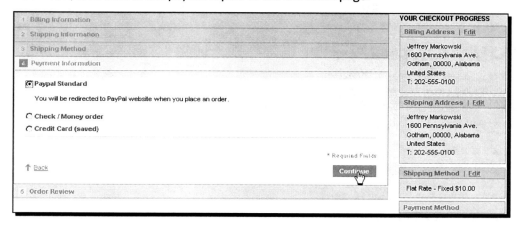

On this page, we give the customer several options for payment. You will learn how to configure Magento to accept payments from **Paypal**, **Check/Money Order**, **Authorize.net**, and **Credit Card(saved)** information.

To keep your customers informed about the progress of their orders, you can generate invoices and shipping notices from Magento. The following is an example of an invoice generated for a customer:

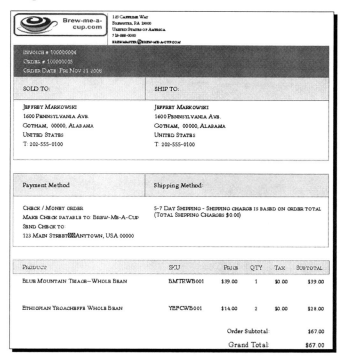

6. This is just a sample of the features that we will work with as we build our store with Magento.

What just happened?

This tour introduced you to Magento's basic features. There is much more that you can do with Magento. The features we demonstrated here are the minimum requirements to make a Magento storefront functional. To make the store's appearance and organization yours, you need to:

◆ Add products
◆ Categorize products
◆ Create a navigation menu
◆ Configure payment options
◆ Configure shipping options
◆ Configure taxes
◆ Customize the front page
◆ Process orders

Summary

In the chapters that follow, we will work in detail with the basic features we saw in this chapter. When we finish, we will have an attractive, functional, and professional storefront. The next chapter deals with Magento installation.

2
Installation

Some hosting companies will install Magento for you, or have a one-click installation for Magento. However, most users will find themselves installing Magento. The process is not any more difficult than most installations of php-based software. However, there are a few points that you must pay close attention to.

This chapter is written especially for you, if you are:

- ◆ Installing Magento on your own
- ◆ Using a low-cost, commonly available hosting service
- ◆ Familiar with putting files up on a web server, but that is the limit of your technical knowledge
- ◆ Willing to ask your hosting service's technical support some simple and specific "Yes/No" questions about their setup
- ◆ Eager to get your store up and running as fast as possible

Even if you own a server, or are very technical, this chapter is still worth reading. It can save you time by helping you to avoid problems while installing Magento.

System requirements

You must install Magento on a web server. There are many kinds of web servers, but Magento is designed to run best in a LAMP environment: Linux, Apache, MySQL, and PHP. It will run on Windows instead of Linux, but with some known issues that the official Magento site discusses. There are many low-cost hosting services that offer all the requirements for a successful Magento installation. Therefore, there is almost no excuse to settle for a service that is missing any of the requirements.

A list of requirements

Here is a short list of what your hosting service must provide. We'll discuss each of these items later.

Requirement	Notes
Linux	Your web server should run Linux. Other Unix-operating systems will also work, as will Windows. However, Linux is so popular among hosting services that you shouldn't settle for anything less than your exact requirement.
Apache web server	As of this writing, the Apache web server is up to version 2.2. However, many hosting services still use the proven, reliable version 1.3. Either will work with Magento.
PHP 5.2.0 or newer	PHP is a scripting language (a type of programming language). PHP is especially suited for web development. PHP code can be embedded into HTML pages to transform a static web page into something dynamic.
	Magento is written in PHP. It is built on the Zend Framework, which means it uses Zend's library. If you want to customize Magento code, you should know not only PHP, but also something about Zend.
	You can take special steps to install Magento on a web server that has only PHP version 4. However, so many hosting services have moved to PHP 5+ that you should not settle for less.

Requirement	Notes
PHP should have the following extensions and add-ons:	PHP's abilities can be increased with extensions and add-ons. The ones listed here are used by Magento, so your hosting service needs to have them installed like almost all hosting services do.
PDO/MySQL mcrypt hash simplexml GD DOM iconv	The easiest way to find out if your hosting service has the version and extensions you need is to ask their technical support department. However, if you want to obtain this information yourself, and you can upload a page to your host (maybe you're already a customer, or are on a trial period), see the next section. If you are setting up a localhost to try Magento, you might be using WAMP from the Apache Friends project. If so, you will also need to install the CURL library.
MySQL 4.1.20 or newer	MySQL is the world's most popular open source database. As of this writing, MySQL is up to version 5.1. Most likely any hosting service you are considering will offer a recent enough version for Magento.
An SMTP server	**SMTP** stands for **Simple Mail Transfer Protocol**. Most email systems use SMTP to send messages from one server to another. When Magento needs to send an email (such as an order confirmation), it connects to your host's SMTP server and the server sends the email on Magento's behalf. Magento can also use a program called Sendmail to send emails. However, only a few hosts offer Sendmail. As almost all hosts offer SMTP, this chapter will deal with SMTP.

Many hosting services advertise LAMP, which covers four of the previous six requirements. Also, a list of their features will show you that they offer SMTP. That covers five of the six requirements. What about the PHP extensions? As stated in the table, the easiest way to find out if your hosting service offers the PHP extensions is to ask the technical support department. However, if you'd like to see for yourself, use the technique covered in the next section.

Determining which PHP version and extensions your web server has

You can see your server's PHP information by uploading and displaying a web page that has the `phpinfo` function.

Create a web page that has just these lines in it, and nothing else:

```php
<?php
phpinfo();
?>
```

Save the file using any name you want, as long as it ends with `.php`, for example `phpinfo.php`.

Point your browser to the page you just created. For example, I pointed my browser to `http://www.brew-me-a-cup.com/phpinfo.php`. The page will look like the following screenshot:

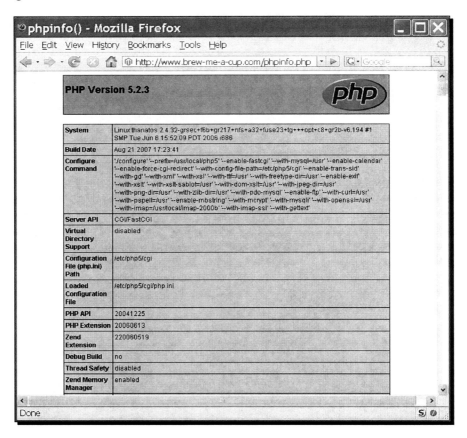

As you scroll down the page, you will see the names of the PHP extensions that have been installed. For example, as you scroll down you will see a section for the DOM extension, which confirms that this extension is installed and working.

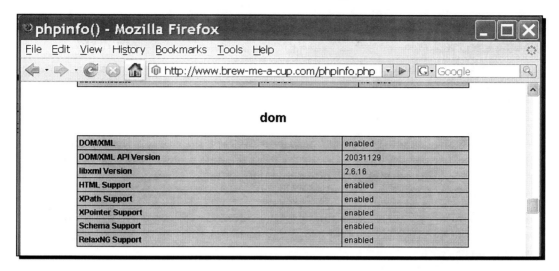

Keep scrolling until you find all the extensions listed in the table of the previous screenshot. Conversely, you can also scroll down to verify that an extension has not been installed on the server. To make it easier to find the extensions, you can search the page for their names. In Firefox, you can use **Edit | Find**, and in Internet Explorer you can use **Edit | Find on This Page**.

Do you have Apache's mod_rewrite and SSL?

Before proceeding with the installation, or even before choosing a hosting service, check with the hosting service to see if they have `mod_rewrite` installed and what it costs to obtain an SSL certificate. Both are explained in the sections that follow.

mod_rewrite makes user-friendly URLs

Compare these two URLs:

```
http://williamrice.com/node/267393?article=123&abc
```

```
http://williamrice.com/magazine/how-to-sell-more-coffee
```

They could both point to the same page. However, the second URL is easier for the user to understand and remember. It enables the user to see where (s)he is on your site (reading and article from the magazine section). Also, this link is easier to send in an email, and doesn't break in the **Favorites** or **Bookmarks** function of your browser. Lastly, search engines usually give better ranking to URLs that do not contain special characters, such as ? and &, and keywords that describe the content of the page.

Magento tends to create URLs like the first one. However, if your hosting service has an Apache module called `mod_rewrite` installed, then you can tell Magento to create friendly URLs like the second one. Check with your hosting service before you begin the Magento installation.

Do you need SSL?

SSL is the standard for secure transactions on the Web. SSL encrypts data—such as credit card numbers—as it travels between your browser and the site you are using. This prevents thieves from stealing that data. When you're on a page protected by SSL, its URL begins with `https://`.

Your browser alone cannot secure the transaction. The web site needs an SSL certificate. The SSL certificate does two things. First, it encrypts the data traveling between the site and your browser. Second, it helps to prove that the site actually belongs to the person who claims to own it.

Obtaining an SSL certificate is beyond the scope of this manual. However, many hosting services will add it to your account for a fee. This means you can just "upgrade" your service to an SSL certificate.

You don't need to decide on using SSL before installing Magento. You can install and configure your online store, and then add SSL later. Also, if you are using a third party such as PayPal, Authorize.net, or Google Checkout to process your payments, then payments will happen on their web site and not yours. They will use their SSL certificate, and you do not need it to protect your customer's credit card accounts.

Give this some serious consideration. Using SSL makes your site more secure. It also might make some people more comfortable about buying from your online store. Sometimes an increase in trust leads to an increase in business. Do your research, and decide if the extra expense is worth the potential increase in business.

Installing Magento

After you confirm that your web host meets the requirements for Magento, you are ready to install the software. The major steps for installing Magento are listed as follows:

1. Download Magento from `http://www.magentocommerce.com`.
2. Upload Magento to your web host.
3. Set rights for some of Magento's directories and files.
4. Create a MySQL database and database user for Magento.

5. Point your browser to the Magento directory and step through the installation wizard.

6. Test the frontend and backend of your Magento site.

After that, you're ready to start with creating your online store! Each of these major steps is covered in the subsections that follow.

Time for action: Downloading Magento

In this section we will download and decompress the Magento files.

1. Getting the Magento files

Point your browser to `http://www.magentocommerce.com/download`. You will see a page like this:

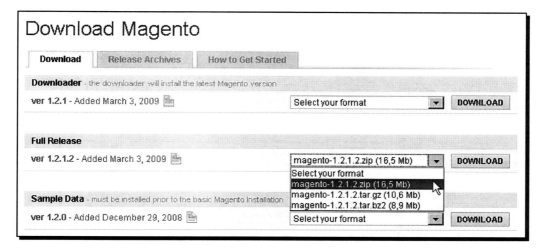

The Magento team provides sample data that we can use if we want to play with Magento. This sample data includes product images and information that will appear on your site. Note that if we want to use this sample data, we must download and install it *before* we install the Magento software. In the next chapter, we will add our own products to Magento. Therefore, we will not need the sample data; we will create our store with our own data.

You can download Magento in several different formats. All of these formats—.zip, .gz, and .bz2—are just different ways of compressing files so that they occupy less space.

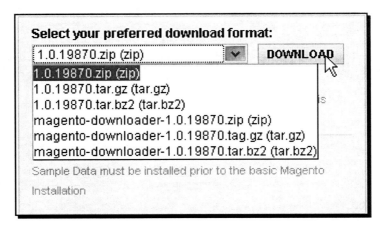

I chose to download the .zip file and save it to my local hard drive. Notice that I did *not* choose to decompress (that is, to unzip) the file. Choosing that option would decompress the file while it's getting downloaded. Instead, I saved the .zip file intact to my computer:

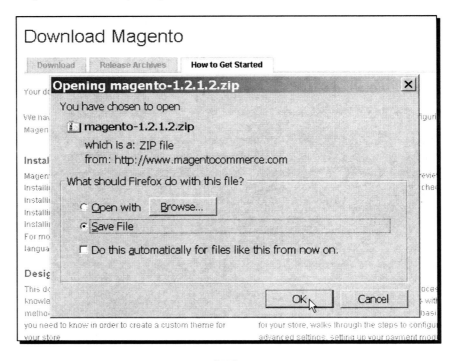

I'll decompress the file later. However, I want the original ZIP file on my local hard drive, just in case I need it again. And, I have found that compressed files usually download faster and more reliably when you save them intact and decompress them after downloading, instead of decompressing them while they download.

2. Decompressing the Magento archive

I chose to download the .zip file because Mac OS X and Windows XP/Vista have built-in support for opening compressed .zip archives. Also, many Linux distributions, such as Ubuntu, have built-in support for .zip archives.

The next step is to decompress the .zip archive. In Windows, you can right-click on the file and select **Extract All,** as shown in the following screenshot:

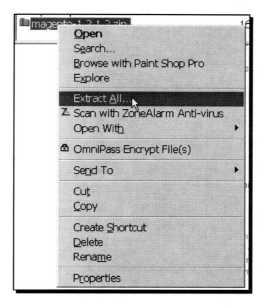

On Mac OS X, you can right-click or Control-click on the file and select **Open With | Archive Utility** like this:

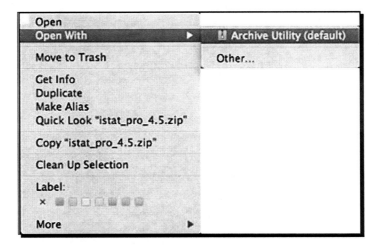

The result should be a folder on your local hard drive called magento, with subfolders that you will upload:

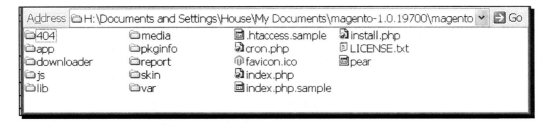

In the next step you will upload these folders to your site. But before you do that, let me explain why you decompressed the Magento archive on your local hard drive.

Many web hosts enable you to decompress a ZIP file that you upload to the host. For example, using the popular Control Panel software, I uploaded the Magento ZIP file to a web host.

I then selected the `.zip` file.

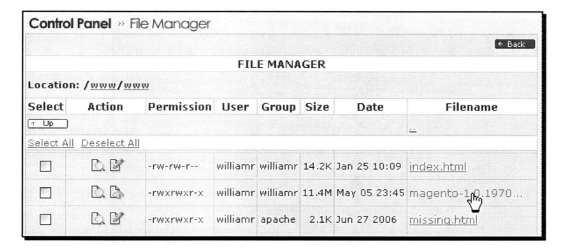

The host then offered to unzip the file for me. This capability is a part of most web hosting services.

The result is a subdirectory on my web site called `magento`, with all of the Magento files placed inside.

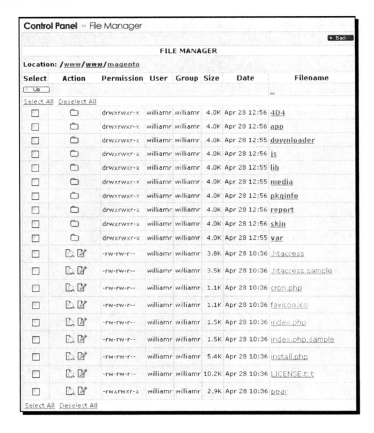

Again, it unzipped the files into a subdirectory, not the root directory of my web site. That meant when customers access my storefront, they would go to `http://williamrice.com/magento`. However, I want my customers to simply go to `http://williamrice.com`.

To do this, I would need to unzip the files on my local computer and upload them, so that I can control which directory they appear in. I don't want the ZIP file to create a subdirectory for Magento. Instead, I want to place the Magento files in the root directory of my site. That's why I unzip the file on my local computer and upload the individual files to my site.

What just happened?

At this point, you have all of the Magento files on your computer ready to be uploaded to your web host. The files are unzipped, so you can see how the files are organized into folders.

Time for action: Uploading Magento to your web host

1. Upload the unzipped files from the `magento` folder to your web host. I used a freeware FTP client called WinSCP, which you can get from `http://winscp.net`.

2. Notice that I uploaded the files to the root directory of `http://brew-me-a-cup.com`, so that visitors see my storefront as soon as they come to the site.

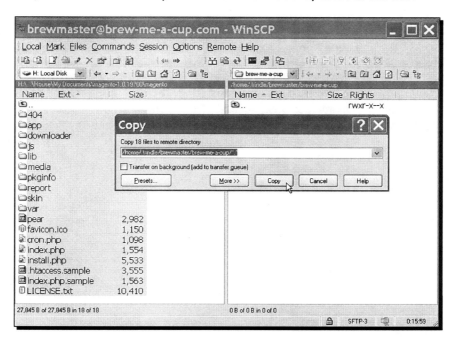

3. The following is a screenshot of the store's root directory after all the Magento files have been uploaded:

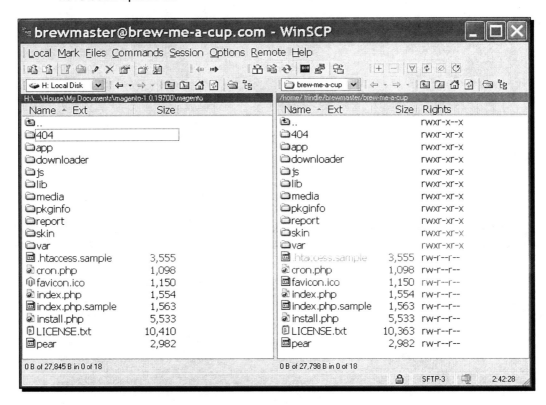

4. If you're installing Magento on a localhost, then the root directory will be the `htdocs` folder. On my localhost, I used XAMPP from Apache Friends to run Apache, MySQL, and PHP. In the `xampp` folder, the folder `htdocs` holds my web files:

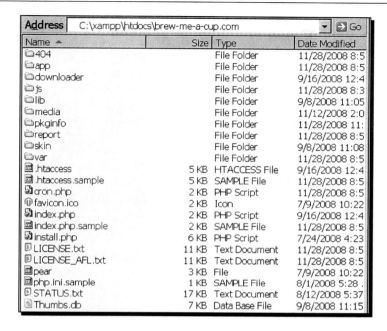

5. When I run Magento on my localhost, I will point my web browser to `http://localhost/brew-me-a-cup.com`.

What just happened?

The Magento files now reside in you web host. If you're running Magento on a local host, the files now reside in the `htdocs` directory.

Setting rights (permissions) for some of Magento's directories and files

I am assuming that you are installing Magento on a Linux host because that is the recommended method. On a Linux host, every directory and file has a set of permissions. In the next three subsections, let's go over the basics of file permissions in Linux. Then, we will set the correct file permissions for our Magento files.

About owners and groups

A Linux web host almost always has multiple users. This is called a shared host because users share the computer's resources.

Every user will belong to one or more group(s). A group enables the administrator of that computer to manage a group of users at once. For example, suppose all customers using the computer as a web server are in a group called Webusers. Also, suppose the company that owns the server decides to increase the amount of space they give to each of their customers. Then, the administrator of the computer can increase the space for all the customers at once, just by increasing the space for the group Webusers. As a customer of a shared hosting service, you will be in a user group.

On a Linux host, every file and directory has an owner. The owner is one of the users on that computer. For example, you are the owner of the files that you upload to the host. Every file also belongs to a group. In the following screenshot, you can see that **brewmaster** is the owner of all files and directories that were uploaded to the store's directory. You can also see that all of the files and directories belong to a group called **pg1404808**. The name of that group doesn't mean anything to you as a user. It was assigned by the hosting service.

Name ▲ Ext	Owner	Group	Rights	Size
/home/.trindle/brewmaster/brew-me-a-cup				
..	brewmaster	pg1404808	rwxr-x--x	
404	brewmaster	pg1404808	rwxr-xr-x	
app	brewmaster	pg1404808	rwxr-xr-x	
downloader	brewmaster	pg1404808	rwxr-xr-x	
js	brewmaster	pg1404808	rwxr-xr-x	
lib	brewmaster	pg1404808	rwxr-xr-x	
media	brewmaster	pg1404808	rwxrwxrwx	
pkginfo	brewmaster	pg1404808	rwxr-xr-x	
report	brewmaster	pg1404808	rwxr-xr-x	
skin	brewmaster	pg1404808	rwxr-xr-x	
store	brewmaster	pg1404808	rwxr-xr-x	
var	brewmaster	pg1404808	rwxrwxrwx	
.htaccess	brewmaster	pg1404808	rw-r--r--	3,555
.htaccess.sample	brewmaster	pg1404808	rw-r--r--	3,555
cron.php	brewmaster	pg1404808	rw-r--r--	1,098
favicon.ico	brewmaster	pg1404808	rw-r--r--	1,150
index.php	brewmaster	pg1404808	rw-r--r--	1,554
index.php.sample	brewmaster	pg1404808	rw-r--r--	1,563
install.php	brewmaster	pg1404808	rw-r--r--	5,533
LICENSE.txt	brewmaster	pg1404808	rw-r--r--	10,363
pear	brewmaster	pg1404808	rw-r--r--	2,982
phpinfo.php	brewmaster	pg1404808	rw-r--r--	22

About rights

In the previous screenshot, you may have noticed the column labeled **Rights**. This column tells you what the user, group, and other users on the server are allowed to do with a file. For example, look at the directory **404**. Notice that there are nine characters in the **Rights** column for that directory: **rwxr-xr-x**. The *first three* characters tell you what the owner is allowed to do with this directory or file. The *next three* tell you what the group is allowed to do. The *last three* tell you what other users on this server are allowed to do with the directory or file. So, the rights can be broken down like this:

owner: **rwx**, group: **r-x**, and other users: **r-x**

The **rwx** tells you that the owner of this directory, **brewmaster**, is allowed to read, write, and execute this directory. After that, the **r-x** tells you that the group to which this file belongs, **pg1404808**, is allowed to read and execute this directory. However, the group cannot write this directory, which means it cannot edit, rename, or delete it. Lastly, the second **r-x** tells you that other users on this computer can also read and execute the directory.

Using numbers (octals) to state permissions

As you saw, you can use a series of nine letters to express the rights that a directory or file has. The example we used was the directory **404**, which has the rights **rwxr-xr-x**. You can also express the rights for a file or directory using a three-digit number. In the following screenshot, look at the field labelled **Octal** and note the number **755** in that field:

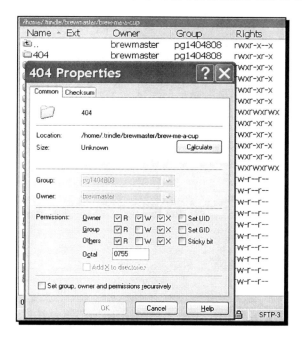

When you set permissions for a file, you will use your FTP application or web host's control panel to specify those permissions. In this case, you can see that the FTP application I use, WinSCP, enables me to state the file permissions as either letters (**rwxr-xr-x**), or as a number (**755**). Not every application gives you both options. Some applications force you to specify file permissions using letters, while others force you to use a number. Therefore, you should know how to express file permissions using both.

Let's look at this example again. We can see that the file permissions **rwxr-xr-x** are equivalent to the file permissions **755**. So, we can deduce the following:

> rwx = 7
>
> r-x = 5

Here is the complete list of permissions expressed in both letters and numbers. Remember that the permissions for a file or directory will consist of three sets of these rights—one for the owner, one for the group, and one for all other users:

Letters	Number	Meaning
- - x	1	The user can execute the file, but cannot read or write it
- w -	2	The user can write (change, rename, and delete) the file, but cannot read or execute it
- w x	3	The user can write and execute the file, but cannot read it
r - -	4	The user can only read the file
r – x	5	The user can read and execute the file, but cannot write (change, rename, and delete) it
r w -	6	The user can read and write the file, but cannot execute it
r w x	7	The user can do anything with the file

In the following screenshot, I am setting the permissions for the file **index.html** on my web site. I am using the web-based control panel provided by my hosting service. Notice that I must specify the **permissions** using numbers. Also, notice that this control panel allows me to choose only some **permissions**. For example, they do not allow the permission 777, which would allow anyone who gains access to the host complete control of that file.

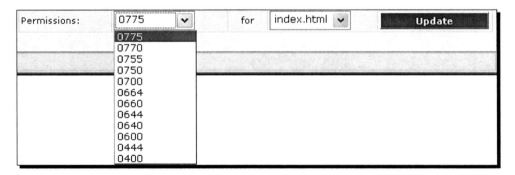

Now that you have learned a little about file permissions on a Linux server, you know that:

◆ A Linux host usually has many users

◆ Every file and directory has an owner and belongs to a group

- For every file and directory, there is a set of permissions that specify what the owner, group, and all other users of that server can do with the file or directory

- You are concerned mostly with what an owner and all others can do with a file

- The permissions for a file or directory can be expressed as nine letters (three groups of three), or as three digits

- You will use your FTP application, or the web-based control panel provided by your hosting service, to set file and directory permissions

Let's move on and set the proper permissions for Magento's files and directories.

Time for action: Setting the rights

1. Using your FTP program, or your hosting service's web-based control panel, set the permissions for the following files and directories to rwxrwxrwx, or 777:

   - **/var/.htaccess** (file)
   - **/app/etc** (directory)
   - **/var** (another directory)
   - All the directories under **/media**

   Notice that you are changing the permissions for the directories and all of the files under those directories. This is called making the permissions **recursive**. You might see that option in the FTP application when you set these permissions.

2. With my FTP application, I set permissions by right-clicking on the file or folder and selecting **Properties** from the pop-up menu, as shown in the following screenshot:

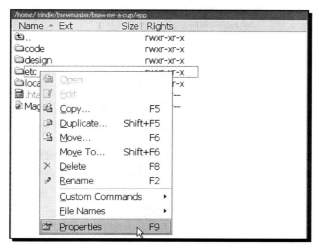

3. In the resulting window, I can set permissions using letters or numbers:

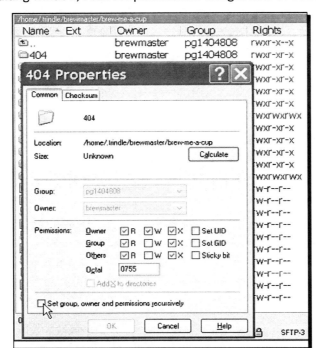

4. Remember to make the permissions recursive.

 If you are installing Magento on a Windows PC, you don't need to set permissions. However, you will need to set permissions when you move your Magento installation from your Windows PC to a Linux host.

What just happened?

If you installed Magento on a Linux host, the permissions for the files should now be set. Files that the public (your users) should not be able to access or change are now protected.

Time for action : Creating a database and database user

In this step, we will create a MySQL database where Magento will store the information that you add about your products, transactions, and customer information. We will also create a username and password for that database. Later, we will enter the database's name, location, username, and password into Magento. This will enable Magento to connect to that database.

The process for creating a database and user varies by the hosting service. I will show a method that is common to many hosting services. However, you should always check with your hosting service before proceeding with this step.

Using cPanel to create a database and a database user

1. Like many hosting services, the one I use for this demonstration offers the cPanel **control panel**. cPanel is web-based, so you don't need to install anything on your computer to use it. Using your web browser, you just log into your hosting service using the username and password they provide to you.

2. From the cPanel **Home Page**, I select **MySQL Databases**.

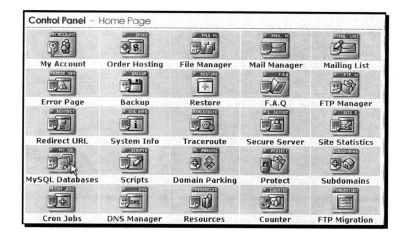

3. Then, I enter the name of the database and click on the **Create** button.

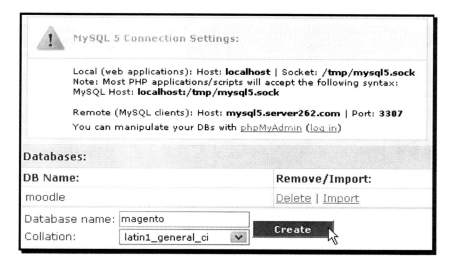

4. The previous screenshot contains some very important information that I will need later.

5. For Magento to connect to this database, it must know:

   ❑ Where to find the MySQL host

   ❑ The name of the database

   ❑ The username and password of a user who has access to that database

6. Notice the name of the MySQL host, **localhost:/tmp/mysql5.sock**. This is where an application that is located on the same server will find the MySQL host. It is one of the parameters that I will enter into Magento. I will also need the name of the database—in this case, **magento**.

7. Now, I will create a user for this database. I've selected **magento** as the username, and I will give that user all privileges on that database:

8. Using cPanel, this is all I need to create a database and a database user for Magento.

Using DreamHost to create a database and a database user

1. I will also demonstrate creating a database and a database user on a hosting service that does not use cPanel. This demonstration is done on http://www.dreamhost.com/. This is not an endorsement of their hosting service. I chose them for this demonstration because their process is different from most, and thus offers a different perspective on this task. You will see that even though the keystrokes and clicks are very different, the basic principles are the same.

2. On the previous hosting service, the MySQL host name was assigned by the hosting service. On DreamHost, I create a MySQL host name. See the field **New Hostname** in the following screenshot:

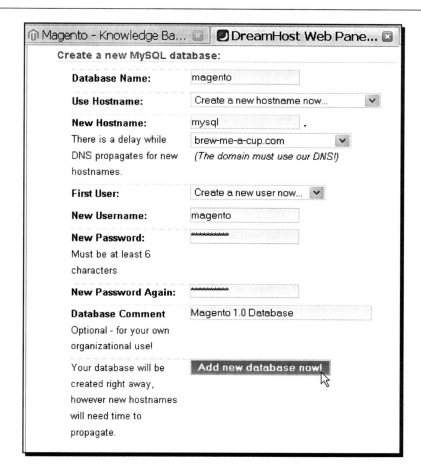

3. In this case, I called the MySQL host **mysql**. I must create the MySQL host on a domain that I own, and so I used **brew-me-a-cup.com**. The result is that when I enter the database host name into Magento, I will enter **mysql.brew-me-a-cup.com**.

4. I also specify the database name, user, and password in this screen. That part is the same as the previous hosting service.

5. Here is the confirmation message for creating this database:

```
✓ Success!

Your database "magento" has been created!

Your hostname "mysql.brew-me-a-cup.com" will be set up within about
5-10 minutes.
You MUST always use your hostname to connect to your database...
"localhost" WILL NOT WORK.

Connect to your new database from the command line with:
mysql -u magento -p -h mysql.brew-me-a-cup.com magento
You can also go to http://mysql.brew-me-a-cup.com/ to manage your
MySQL database from the web (once the hostname is set up of course).
```

Localhost

1. If you are installing Magento on a localhost, you can probably use phpMyAdmin to create the database and user. For example, XAMPP and WAMP both include phpMyAdmin in their products. This process is well-documented at many web sites.

What just happened?

From the examples that we discussed, you can see that creating a database on your hosting service will always involve a few steps:

1. Choose a name for the database.

2. Create a user with full rights to the database.

3. Give the user a secure password.

4. Create or determine a host name for the MySQL host.

Most good hosting services offer detailed directions that will help you to accomplish these steps quickly and easily.

You now have a database for Magento to use. That database resides on your hosting service, or on your localhost. A username has been created for that database. In the next section, you will tell Magento which username and database to use.

Time for action: Pointing your browser to the Magento directory and stepping through the installation wizard

1. Point your browser to Magento's **install** directory. For example, I installed Magento at **brew-me-a-cup.com**. So I point my browser to **brew-me-a-cup.com/install**. If you installed in the root directory of a localhost, you would point your browser to `http://localhost/magento/index.php/install/`. This begins an installation routine. The first step is to confirm the software license.

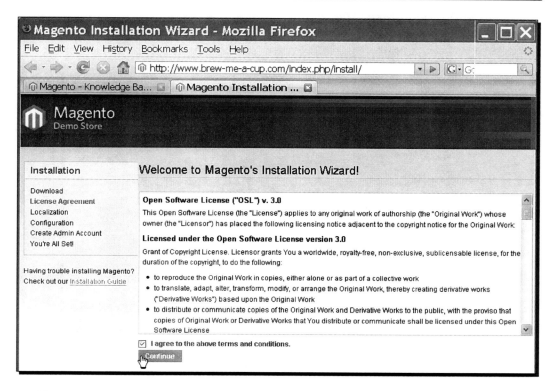

2. Next, select the **Locale**, **Time Zone**, and **Default Currency**. Note that you are selecting the default language and currency. Magento can work with multiple languages and currencies, but that is beyond the scope of this beginner's guide. First, let's get the basic store working.

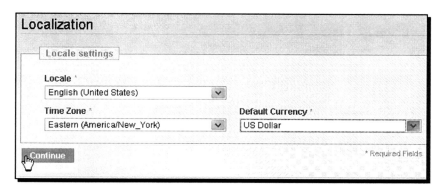

3. Next, enter the database information that you collected while creating the database and the database user.

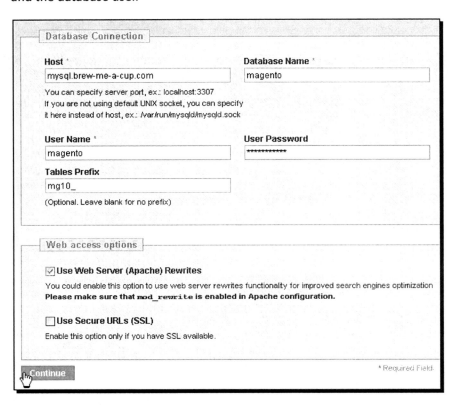

4. Notice that I've select the checkbox for **Use Web Server (Apache) Rewrites**. This will create more user-friendly URLs for the web pages in my store, and might make them rank better in search engines.

5. Next, you will need to create an administrator account for your Magento system. You should save all of the information from this screen in a safe place. I put mine into an email that I sent myself, in an encrypted document on my Smart Phone, and also stored a hard copy in a safe place.

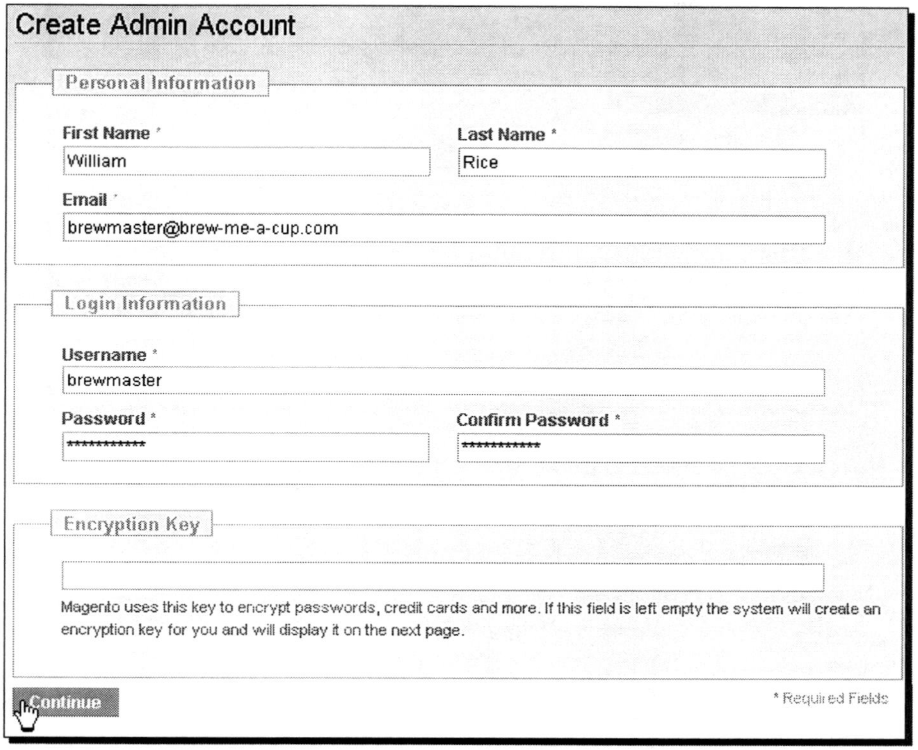

Create Admin Account

Personal Information

First Name *
William

Last Name *
Rice

Email *
brewmaster@brew-me-a-cup.com

Login Information

Username *
brewmaster

Password *
****

Confirm Password *
****

Encryption Key

Magento uses this key to encrypt passwords, credit cards and more. If this field is left empty the system will create an encryption key for you and will display it on the next page.

Continue

* Required Fields

6. You can leave the **Encryption Key** field blank. Just remember to record the key that is displayed in the following screenshot:

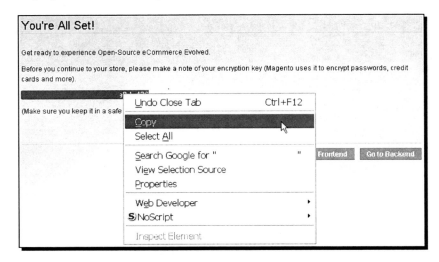

7. Now, go to your site's frontend. This is the page that your shoppers will see. When I did this, I saw the following error message:

8. This is one of the most common errors with a Magento installation. It is not unique to Magento. Many PHP applications experience this error. There are several solutions that will clear this up. In the given order, try these:

- ❑ Make sure that your hosting service uses PHP version 5.

- ❑ In your root directory, there might be a file called `php.ini`. If so, rename it to `php5.ini`. If you see files with names such as `.alias`, `.bash_profile`, `.cshrc`, `.screenrc`, you are looking at the root directory. If you're unsure, ask your hosting service.

- ❑ If that doesn't work, add the line `cgi.fix_pathinfo = 1` to the end of `php5.ini`.

- ❑ If that doesn't work, add the line `Options -MultiViews` to the top of the file named `.htaccess`.

- ❑ If that doesn't work, search the knowledge base and forums at `http://magentocommerce.com` for help.

9. If your site's frontend works properly, you should see something like this:

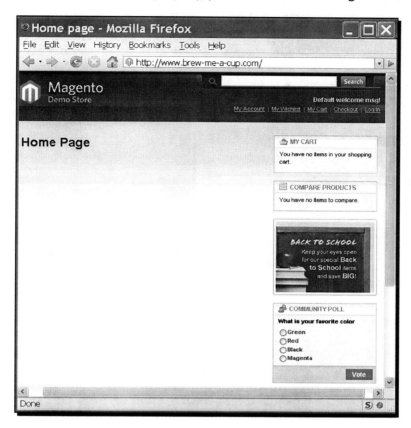

10. To visit your site's backend, go to your Magento home page and add `/admin`, as done in the following screenshot:

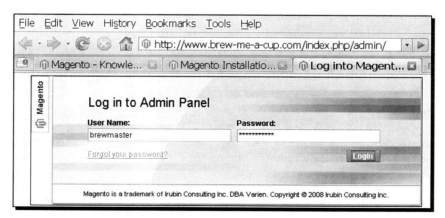

11. After logging in to your site's backend, you will see the **Admin Panel**.

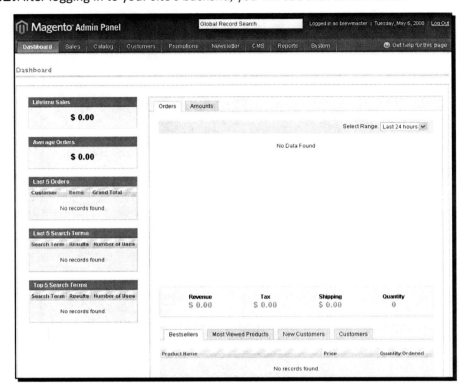

12. Congratulations! You have a working Magento store.

What just happened?

Installing Magento is very similar to installing most PHP-based applications. You first set up your Apache-MySQL-PHP environment, or confirm that your hosting service has the right environment. Then you download, unzip, and upload Magento. You set permissions, and create a database and a database user. Finally, you step through the installation wizard. The result is a fully functional Magento system that is ready to be customized into your storefront.

Configuring a store without having some products in place is like formatting an empty word processing document. You just can't see the effect of your choices unless you have some products in place. However, Magento does offer some sample data that you can load directly into its database. There are directions for that on the official Magento web site. Keep in mind, using their products will not teach you how to add your own products. Also, you will need to start adding your own products eventually. In the next chapter, we will start adding some products to your store.

Check

Perform the following check before proceeding to the next chapter:

◆ Does your hosting service have all of the prerequisites listed in this chapter?

◆ Have you emailed your hosting service's technical support department and confirmed this?

◆ Have others successfully installed Magento on the hosting service that you are considering to use? Get onto the Magneto discussion boards and check.

◆ Do you have an FTP client for uploading your files? Also, do you have a good text editor?

If all of your answers are "Yes," then you're ready to install.

Summary

The hosting requirements for Magento can be met by many hosting services. Be choosy. Pick one that offers all of the requirements, is reliable, and gives you the ability to set the file permissions that you need. The Magento message board is a good place to ask other users about their experiences with hosting services.

In this chapter, we examined the process for installing Magento. We prepared our hosting environment, uploaded Magento, and stepped through the installer. You might want to try this on your local computer (localhost) before trying it on a hosting service. Doing this enables you to experiment with your store, and learn Magento without the fear of ruining your store.

3
Categories and Attributes

The combination of products, presentation, and service makes our store unique. In this chapter, we will see how to add products to our store. Before adding products, we need to make some decisions about how we will organize our site. A few minutes of planning now can save us hours of work later.

Categories, Products, and Attributes

Products are the items that are sold. In Magento, **Categories** organize your Products, and **Attributes** describe them. Think of a Category as the place where a Product lives, and an Attribute is anything that describes a Product. Each one of your Products can belong to one or more Categories. Also, each Product can be described by any number of Attributes.

Is it a Category or an Attribute?

Some things are clearly Categories. For example, if you have an electronics store, MP3 players would make a good Category. If you're selling jewelry, earrings would make a good Category.

Other things are clearly Attributes. Color, description, picture, and SKU number are almost always Attributes.

Sometimes, the same thing can be used for a Category or an Attribute. For example, suppose your site sells shoes. If you made size an Attribute, then after your shoppers have located a specific shoe, they can select the size they want. However, if you also made size a Category, the shoppers could begin their shopping by selecting their size. Then they could browse through the styles available in their size. So should size be an Attribute, a Category, or both? The answer depends upon what kind of shopping experience you want to create for your customers.

Examples

The hierarchy of Categories, Products, and Attributes looks like this:

- Category 1
    - Product 1
        - Attribute 1
        - Attribute 2
    - Product 2
        - Attribute 1
        - Attribute 2

- Category 2
    - Product 3
        - Attribute 1
        - Attribute 3
    - Product 4
        - Attribute 1
        - Attribute 3

We are building a site that sells gourmet coffee, so we might organize our store like this:

- Single Origin
    - Hawaiian Kona
        - Grind (whole bean, drip, French press)
        - Roast (light, medium, dark)
    - Blue Mountain
        - Grind
        - Roast

- Blends
    - Breakfast Blend
        - Grind
        - Caffeine (regular, decaffeinated)
    - Afternoon Cruise
        - Grind
        - Caffeine

In Magento, you can give your shoppers the ability to search your store. So if the shoppers know that they want Blue Mountain coffee, they can use the **Search** function to find it in our store. However, customers who don't know exactly what they want will browse the store. They will often begin browsing by selecting a category. With the organization that we just saw, when customers browse our store, they will start by selecting Single Origin or Blends. Then the shoppers will select the product they want: Hawaiian Kona, Blue Mountain, Breakfast Blend, or Afternoon Cruise.

After our shoppers decide upon a Product, they select Attributes for that product. In our store, shoppers can select Grind for any of the products. For Single Origin, they can also select Roast. For blends, they can select Caffeine. This gives you a clue about how Magento handles attributes. To each Product, you can apply as many, or as few, attributes as you want.

Now that we have definitions for Category, Product, and Attribute, let's look at each of them in detail. Then, we can start adding products.

Categories

Product Categories are important because they are the primary tool that your shoppers use to navigate your store. Product Categories organize your store for your shoppers. Categories can be organized into Parent Categories and Subcategories. To get to a Subcategory, you drill down through its Parent Category.

Categories and the Navigation Menu

If a Category is an **Anchor Category**, then it appears on the Navigation Menu. The term "Anchor" makes the category sound as if it must be a top-level category. This is not true. You can designate any category as an Anchor Category. Doing so puts that category into the Navigation Menu.

When a shopper selects a normal Category from the Navigation Menu, its landing page and any subcategories are displayed. When a shopper selects an Anchor Category from the menu, Magento does not display the normal list of subcategories. Instead, it displays the Attributes of all the Products in that category and its subcategories. Instead of moving down into subcategories, the shopper uses the Attributes to filter all the Products in that Anchor Category and the Categories below it. The Navigation Menu will **not** display if:

◆ You don't create any Categories, or

◆ You create Categories, but you don't make any of them Anchors, or

◆ Your Anchor Categories are not subcategories under the Default Category.

The Navigation Menu will display *only* if:

- You have created at least one Category
- You have made at least one Category an Anchor
- You have made the Anchor Category a Subcategory under **Default**.

When you first create your Magento site and add Products, you won't see those Products on your site until you've met all of the previous conditions. For this reason I recommend that you create at least one Anchor Category before you start adding Products to your store. As you add each Product, add it to an Anchor Category. Then, the Product will display in your store, and you can preview it. If the Anchor Category is not the one that you want for that Product, you can change the Product's Category later.

Before we add Products to our coffee store, we will create two Anchor Categories: Single Origin and Blends. As we add Products, we will assign them to a Category so that we can preview them in our storefront.

Making best use of Categories

There are three things that Categories can accomplish. They can:

1. Help the shoppers, who know exactly what they want, to find the product that they are looking for.
2. Help the shoppers, who almost know what they want, to find a product that matches their desires.
3. Entice the shoppers, who have almost no idea of what they want, to explore your store.

We would like to organize our store so that our Categories accomplish all these goals. However, these goals are often mutually exclusive.

For example, suppose you create an electronics store. In addition to many other products, your store sells MP3 players, including Apple iPods. A Category called **iPods** would help the shoppers who know that they want an iPod, as they can quickly find one. However, the **iPods** Category doesn't do much to help shoppers who know that they want an MP3 player, but don't know what kind.

On the Web, you usually search something when you know what you want. But when you're not sure about what you want, you usually browse. In an online store, you usually begin browsing by selecting a Category. When you are creating Categories for your online store, try to make them helpful for shoppers who almost know what they want.

However, what if a high percentage of your shoppers are looking for a narrow category of products? Consider creating a top-level Category to make those products easily accessible. Again, suppose you have an electronics store that sells a wide variety of items. If a high percentage of your customers want iPods, it might be worthwhile to create a Category just for those few products. The logs from the *Search* function on your site are one way you can determine whether your shoppers are interested in a narrow Category of a Product. Are 30 percent of the searches on your site for lefthanded fishing reels? If so, you might want to create a top-level Category just for those Products.

Attributes

An Attribute is a characteristic of a Product. Name, price, SKU, size, color, and manufacturer are all examples of Attributes.

System versus Simple Attributes

Notice that the first few examples (name, price, and SKU) are all required for a Product to function in Magento. Magento adds these Attributes to every product, and requires you to assign a value for each of them. These are called **System Attributes**.

The other three examples (size, color, and manufacturer) are optional Attributes. They are created by the store owner. They are called **Simple Attributes**. When we discuss creating and assigning Attributes, we are almost always discussing Simple Attributes.

Attribute Sets

Notice that the Single Origin coffees have two Attributes: Grind and Roast. Also notice that the blends have the Attributes of Grind and Caffeine.

- ◆ Single Origin
    - ❑ Hawaiian Kona
        Grind (whole bean, drip, French press)
        Roast (light, medium, dark)

    - ❑ Blue Mountain
        Grind
        Roast

- ◆ Blends
    - ❑ Breakfast Blend
        Grind
        Caffeine (regular, decaffeinated)
    - ❑ Afternoon Cruise
        Grind
        Caffeine

In this example, the store owner created three Attributes: Grind, Roast, and Caffeine. Next, the store owner grouped the Attributes into two Attribute Sets: one set contains Grind and Roast, and the other set contains Grind and Caffeine. Then, an Attribute set was applied to each Product.

Attributes are not applied directly to Products. They are first grouped into Attribute Sets, and then a set can be applied to a Product. This means that you will need to create a set for each different combination of Attributes in your store. You can name these Sets after the Attributes they contain, such as Grind-Roast. Or, you can name them after the type of Product which will use those Attributes, such as Single Origin Attributes.

If each Product in a group will use the same Attribute as every other Product in that group, then you can name the set after that group. For example, at this time, all Single Origin coffees have the same Attributes: Grind and Roast. If they will all have these two Attributes and you will always add and remove Attributes to them as a group, then you could name the set Single Origin Attributes.

If the Products in a group will likely use different Attributes, then name the set after the Attributes. For example, if you expect that some Single Origin coffees will use the Attributes Grind and Roast, while others will use just Roast, then it would not make sense to create a set called Single Origin Attributes. Instead, create a set called Grind-Roast, and another called Roast.

Three types of Products

In Magento, you can create three different types of Products: Simple, Configurable, and Grouped. The following is a very brief definition for each type of Product.

Simple Product

A **Simple Product** is a single Product, with Attributes that the store owner chooses. As the saying goes, "What you see is what you get." The customer does not get to choose anything about the Product.

In our coffee store, a good example for a Simple Product might be a drip coffee maker. It comes in only one color. And while the customer can buy drip coffee makers of various sizes (4 cups, 8 cups, 12 cups, and so on), each of those is a separate Product.

A bad example of a Simple Product would be a type of coffee. For example, we might want to allow the customer to choose the type of roast for our Hawaiian Kona coffee: light, medium, or dark. Because we want the customer to choose a value for an Attribute, that would not be a good Simple Product.

Configurable Product

A **Configurable Product** is a single Product, with at least one Attribute that the customer gets to choose. There is a saying that goes, "Have it your way." The customer gets to choose something about the Product.

A good example of a Configurable Product would be a type of coffee that comes in several different roasts: light, medium, and dark. Because we want the customer to choose the roast (s)he wants, that would be a good Configurable Product.

Grouped Product

A **Grouped Product** is several Simple Products that are displayed on the same page. You can force the customer to buy the group, or allow the customer to buy each Product separately.

The previous definitions are adequate for now. However, when you start creating Products, you will need to know more about each type of Product. When we discuss Products later in this book, you will learn more about each of these.

Putting it together

In the previous sections, we covered the definitions of Product, Category, and Attribute. A Product appears when it is assigned to an active Category, and that Category is an Anchor, or is under an Anchor Category. Attributes are added to sets, and a set can then be applied to a Product.

I recommend that before you add Products to your store, you create the Anchor Categories into which you will place those Products. This enables you to preview how those Products will appear in your store. I also recommend that you create the Attribute Sets you will need for those Products.

Let's put these concepts into action. In our new store, we will:

1. Create some Anchor Categories.
2. Create some Attribute Sets.
3. Add a few Products.

Time for action: Creating Categories

In this section, we will create a Category for our store. We will make it an Anchor Category so that customers can search for the Products in this category based on their Attributes.

Before you begin

As Categories are the main tools for organizing your store, it is important to make best use of them. Plan which Categories you want to use. What will make products easiest to find? What will entice potential customers to explore? Also, remember that space in the Navigation Menu is limited. So, choose your Anchor Categories carefully.

The result of the following steps is an Anchor Category. By making slightly different choices, you can also create non-Anchor Categories and Subcategories.

1. Log in to your site's backend, which we call the Administrative Panel:

2. Select **Catalog | Manage Categories**:

Notice that there is already one Category, called **Default**:

You are going to add your new Category under **Default**. Doing this will create a Subcategory. This step is essential, because only those Anchor Categories that are children of the **Default** Category will appear in your Navigation Menu.

 You can add Categories so that they are not under the **Default** Category. They will be at the same level as **Default**. However, only Categories under **Default** will automatically appear in the Navigation Menu. If a Category is not under **Default**, you will need to create some other way for your customers to get to that Category.

For example, look at these Categories. Notice that **Single Origin Coffees** is under **Default**, while **I don't appear in the Nav Menu** is not:

The result will be a Navigation Menu with only **Single Origin Coffees** displayed:

3. Select the **Default** Category.

4. Click on **Add Subcategory**. A blank, **New Category** window is displayed:

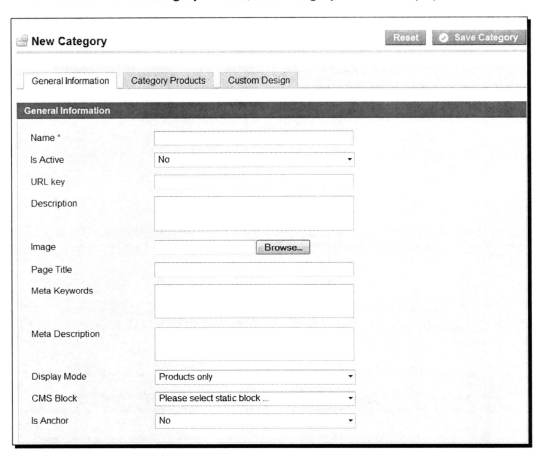

5. Enter a **Name** for the Category. This will display in your storefront. In our example, we will enter **Single Origin Coffees**:

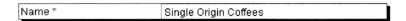

6. For the setting **Is Active**, selecting **Yes** makes the Category visible to customers. Selecting **No** will hide this Category and its Subcategories in your store.

   Because we want this Category to appear in the Navigation Menu, we will select **Yes**.

7. The **URL Key** enables you to enter a search-engine-friendly path for this Category. In this example, I entered **single-origin-coffees** so that when a shopper selects this Category, the address in their browser reads `http://brew-me-a-cup.com`.

   If you leave this field blank, Magento will put the name of the Category into this field. You cannot enter spaces into this field.

8. The **Description** that you enter here will appear on the Category's landing page.

9. The **Image** that you upload will also appear on the Category's landing page. Here is what the page looks like so far:

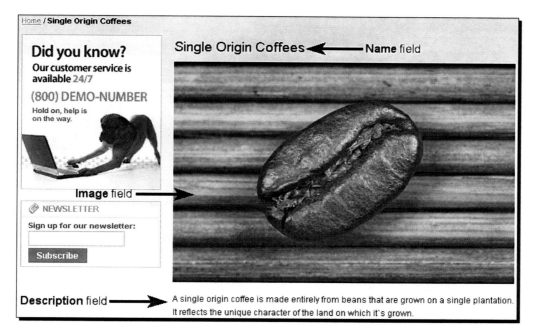

The default Magento template will re-size the Category's image so that it is 475-pixels wide. If you upload an image that is taller than it is wider, the image will take up a lot of space on the landing page. For example, I've uploaded an image that is 240-pixels wide and 266-pixels high. Magento resized the image so that it is 475-pixels wide and 526-pixels high. Notice how much space this image takes up:

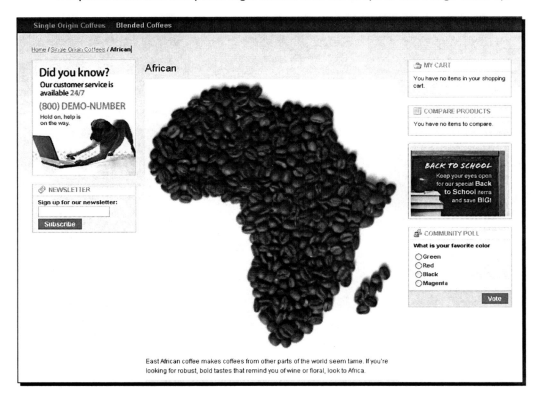

Also notice that the background of the image is solid. It does not allow the gradient on the page to show through. I want an image that will not take up so much vertical space. And, I want the gradient to show through. I solved both problems with this image, which is 475-pixels wide, 266-pixels high, and has a transparent background:

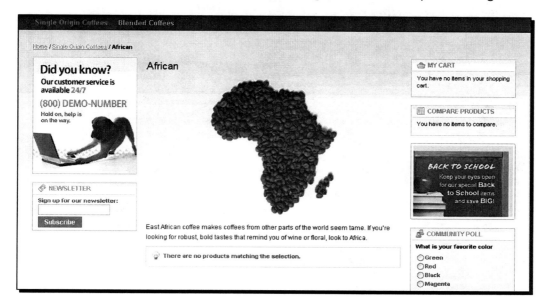

Because the image is already 475-pixels wide, Magento did not re-size it. The result is less space taken up by the image, and more space left for my products.

A full discussion of working with graphic images is beyond the scope of this book. However, here is a hint for creating graphics for your Category landing pages. Design the subject of the graphic according to the size you want. In this example, it was the African continent. Then, make the canvas of the graphic 475-pixels wide. Finally, make the background transparent. The result will be an image that is the right size for your landing page.

10. The **Page Title** appears in the browser's title bar. This is not the same as the **Name**. The **Name** appears in the Navigation Menu at the top of the page, not in the browser's title bar:

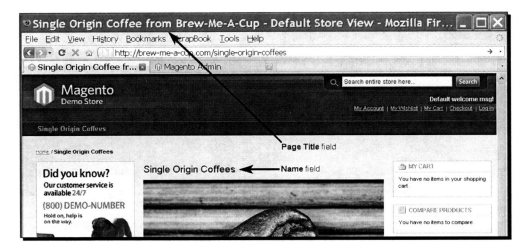

The Category's **Name** and **Page Title** are both opportunities for you to help the page's search engine rank. You can make them identical, which will help the page score better when people search for that term. Or, you can make them different so that both search terms will be covered by this one page.

11. The **Meta Keywords** and **Meta Description** appear in meta tags, in the page's HTML code. Enter information about this page, which you think will help search engines to properly categorize this page.

A meta tag contains information not normally displayed to the user. It contains information about the page. The word "meta" means "about this subject". Webmasters use meta tags to tell search engines about a page and help the search engines better categorize that page.

You can see the meta tags in a page if you view the pages' source code. The following code shows the first few lines of source code for the **Single Origin Coffees** page. Notice the last two meta tags:

```
<!DOCTYPE html PUBLIC "-//W3C//DTD XHTML 1.0 Strict//EN"
"http://www.w3.org/TR/xhtml1/DTD/xhtml1-strict.dtd">
<html xmlns="http://www.w3.org/1999/xhtml" xml:lang="en"
lang="en">
<head>
    <title> Single Origin Coffee from Brew-Me-A-Cup -
Default Store View </title>
<meta http-equiv="Content-Type" content="text/html;
    charset=utf-8"/>
```

```
<meta name="description" content="single origin coffees"/>
<meta name="keywords" content="single origin coffee"/>
```

Use **Meta Keywords** and **Meta Description** as opportunities to optimize the page for search engines.

12. For **Display Mode**, select **Products only**. This will cause the Category's landing page to display a list of products from that Category.

    You can also select **Static block only** or **Static block and products**. We are not selecting these now because we are not covering Static Blocks in this beginner's guide.

13. If we chose to show a Static Block, we would use the **CMS Block** setting to specify which Block to display. For now, we can ignore this setting.

14. We want shoppers to be able to filter products under this Category. So for **Is Anchor**, we will choose **Yes**.

15. Click on the **Save Category** button.

16. This completes the General Information tab for the Category. There are two other tabs: Category Products and Custom Design. We will learn about these tabs later. We have done everything to get this Category to work in our store.

What just happened?

You now have at least one Anchor Category under the Default category. This new Anchor Category has its own landing page, which you customized with text and a graphic. The Products under this Anchor Category will be listed on its landing page.

Have a go hero

Now that we have an Anchor Category, we can press ahead and complete the other steps needed to create our catalog. Or, we can create more Categories. For our coffee store, create several more Categories so that our store is organized like this:

- Single Origin Coffees
    - Latin American
    - African
    - Hawaiian
- Blended Coffees

Single Origin and Blended will be Anchors. The result will look as follows:

Once we have the Categories, we need to hold our Products, it's time to add Attribute Sets.

Time for action: Creating Attributes

In this section we will create an Attribute set for our store. First, we will create Attributes. Then, we will create the set.

Before you begin

Because Attributes are the main tool for describing your Products, it is important to make the best use of them. Plan which Attributes you want to use. What aspects or characteristics of your Products will a customer want to search for? Make those Attributes. What aspects of your Products will a customer want to choose? Make these Attributes, too.

Attributes are organized into Attribute Sets. Each set is a collection of Attributes. You should create different sets to describe the different types of Products that you want to sell. In our coffee store, we will create two Attribute Sets: one for Single Origin coffees and one for Blends. They will differ in only one way. For Single Origin coffees, we will have an Attribute showing the country or region where the coffee is grown. We will not have this Attribute for blends because the coffees used in a blend can come from all over the world. Our sets will look like the following:

Single Origin Attribute set	Blended Attribute set
Name	Name
Description	Description
Image	Image
Grind	Grind
Roast	Roast
Origin	SKU
SKU	Price
Price	Size
Size	

Now, let's create the Attributes and put them into sets.

The result of the following directions will be several new Attributes and two new Attribute Sets:

1. If you haven't already, log in to your site's backend, which we call the Administrative Panel:

2. Select **Catalog | Attributes | Manage Attributes**.

   A list of all the Attributes is displayed. These attributes have been created for you. Some of these Attributes (such as **color**, **cost**, and **description)** are visible to your customers. Other Attributes affect the display of a Product, but your customers will never see them. For example, **custom_design** can be used to specify the name of a custom layout, which will be applied to a Product's page. Your customers will never see the name of the custom layout.

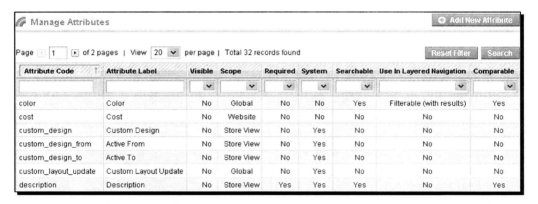

Attribute Code	Attribute Label	Visible	Scope	Required	System	Searchable	Use In Layered Navigation	Comparable
color	Color	No	Global	No	No	Yes	Filterable (with results)	Yes
cost	Cost	No	Website	No	No	No	No	No
custom_design	Custom Design	No	Store View	No	Yes	No	No	No
custom_design_from	Active From	No	Store View	No	Yes	No	No	No
custom_design_to	Active To	No	Store View	No	Yes	No	No	No
custom_layout_update	Custom Layout Update	No	Global	No	Yes	No	No	No
description	Description	No	Store View	Yes	Yes	Yes	No	Yes

   We will add our own attributes to this list.

3. Click the **Add New Attribute** button. The **New Product Attribute** page displays:

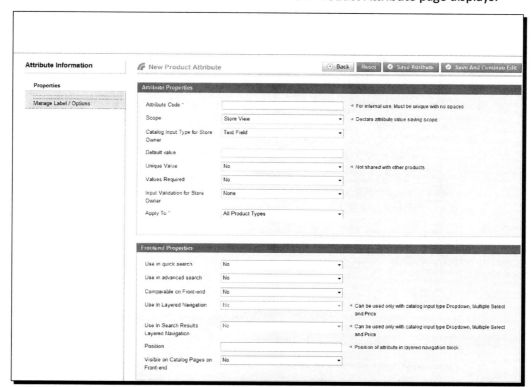

There are two tabs on this page: **Properties** and **Manage Label / Options**. You are in the **Properties** tab.

The **Attribute Properties** section contains settings that only the Magento administrator (you) will see. These settings are values that you will use when working with the Attribute. The **Frontend Properties** section contains settings that affect how this Attribute will be presented to your shoppers. We will cover each setting on this page.

4. **Attribute Code** is the name of the Attribute. Your customers will never see this value. You will use it when managing the Attribute.

Refer back to the list of Attributes that appeared in Step 2. The Attribute identifier appears in the first column, labeled **Attribute Code**. The Attribute Code must contain only lowercase letters, numbers, and the underscore character. And, it must begin with a letter. The **Scope** of this Attribute can be set as **Store View**, **Website**, or **Global**. For now, you can leave it set to the default—**Store View**. The other values become useful when you use one Magento installation to create multiple stores or multiple web sites. That is beyond the scope of this quick-start guide.

5. After you assign an Attribute set to a Product, you will fill in values for the Attributes. For example, suppose you assign a set that contains the attributes color, description, price, and image. You will then need to enter the color, description, price, and image for that Product.

    Notice that each of the Attributes in that set is a different kind of data. For **color**, you would probably want to use a drop-down list to make selecting the right color quick and easy. This would also avoid using different terms for the same color such as "Red" and "Magenta." For description, you would probably want to use a free-form text field. For price, you would probably want to use a field that accepts only numbers, and that requires you to use two decimal places. And for image, you would want a field that enables you to upload a picture.

    The field **Catalog Input Type for Store Owner** enables you to select the kind of data that this Attribute will hold:

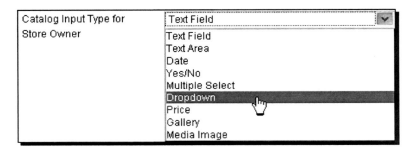

    In our example we are creating an Attribute called **roast**. When we assign this value to a Product, we want to select a single value for this field from a list of choices. So, we will select **Dropdown**.

    If you select **Dropdown** or **Multiple Select** for this field, then under the **Manage Label/Options** tab, you will need to enter the list of choices (the list of values) for this field.

6. If you select **Yes** for **Unique Value**, then no two products can have the same value for this Attribute. For example, if I made **roast** a unique Attribute, that means only one kind of coffee in my store could be a Light roast, only one kind of coffee could be a French roast, only one could be Espresso, and so on. For an Attribute such as **roast**, this wouldn't make much sense. However, if this Attribute was the **SKU** of the Product, then I might want to make it unique. That would prevent me from entering the same SKU number for two different Products.

7. If you select **Yes** for **Values Required**, then you must select or enter a value for this Attribute. You will not be able to save a Product with this Attribute if you leave it blank. In the case of **roast**, it makes sense to require a value. Our customers would not buy a coffee without knowing what kind of roast the coffee has.

8. **Input Validation for Store Owner** causes Magento to check the value entered for an Attribute, and confirm that it is the right kind of data. When entering a value for this Attribute, if you do not enter the kind of data selected, then Magento gives you a warning message.

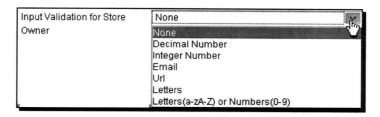

9. The **Apply To** field determines which Product Types can have this Attribute applied to them. Remember that the three Product Types in Magento are Simple, Grouped, and Configurable. Recall that in our coffee store, if a type of coffee comes in only one roast, then it would be a Simple Product. And, if the customer gets to choose the roast, it would be a Configurable Product. So we want to select at least **Simple Product** and **Configurable Product** for the **Apply To** field:

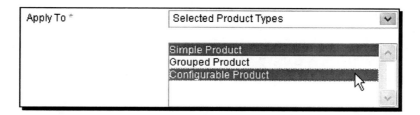

But what about **Grouped Product**? We might sell several different types of coffee in one package, which would make it a Grouped Product. For example, we might sell a Grouped Product that consists of a pound of Hawaiian Kona and a pound of Jamaican Blue Mountain. We could call this group something like "Island Coffees." If we applied the Attribute **roast** to this Grouped Product, then both types of coffee would be required to have the same roast.

However, if Kona is better with a lighter roast and Blue Mountain is better with a darker roast, then we don't want them to have the same roast. So in our coffee store, we will not apply the Attribute **roast** to Grouped Products. When we sell coffees in special groupings, we will select the roast for each coffee.

You will need to decide which Product Types each Attribute can be applied to. If you are the store owner and the only one using your site, you will know which Attributes should be applied to which Products. So, you can safely choose **All Product Types** for this setting.

10. By default, Magento puts a quick search box in the top right corner of each page in your store.

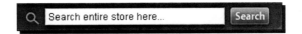

The quick search box will search only those Attributes for which **Use in quick search** is set to **Yes**. For some examples, let's refer back to our list of Attributes:

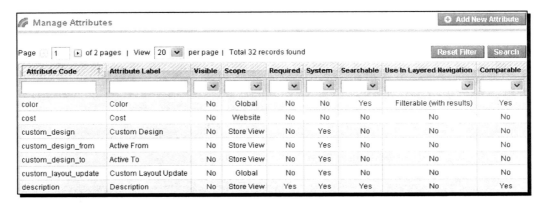

Look in the column labeled **Searchable**. Notice that **color** and **description** are searchable. This means that if a customer enters a word into the quick search box that is found in the **color** or **description** of a Product, then that Product will be found. Notice that customers cannot search based on a Product's **price**.

In our coffee store, we will make **roast** a searchable Attribute because we know that some customers prefer only coffees that are roasted a specific way.

If you select **Yes** for **Use in advanced search**, this attribute will have its own field on the **Advanced Search** page:

In our coffee store, we will make **roast** a field on the **Advanced Search** page.

By default, Magento puts an **Advanced Search** link at the bottom of each page in your store.

Clicking on this link takes you to the **Catalog Advanced Search** page. Some Attributes get their own field on this search page:

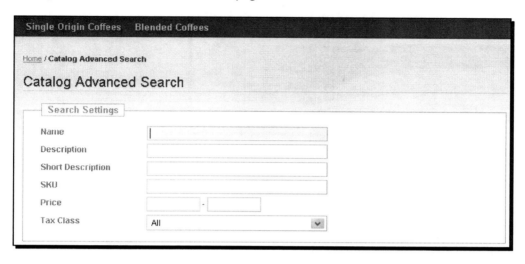

11. By default, Magento enables customers to compare Products in your store. When viewing a Product, the customer sees an **Add to Compare** link, as shown in the following screenshot:

When a customer clicks on this link, the Product is added to the Compare Products block.

Next, when the customer clicks on the **Compare Items** button, the **Compare Products** page pops up:

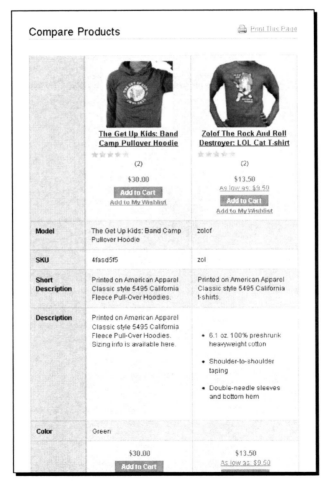

On the **Compare Products** page, notice that only certain Attributes are compared. In the previous example, **Model, SKU, Short Description, Description, Color,** and **Price** appear on the Compare Products page.

If you select **Yes** for **Comparable on Front-end**, this attribute will appear on the Compare Products page.

You don't want to crowd the **Compare Products** page with Attributes, but you want to include all the Attributes that will help your customer to choose between similar Products. This requires you to think like a customer. When your customer is comparing similar Products, which Attributes will help the customer to see a real difference between them?

For example, in our coffee store, customers who are interested in one lightly roasted coffee are probably interested in other light roasts. Any coffees that our customers compare probably have the same roast. Therefore, roast would not be an Attribute that helps our customers to decide between similar Products. So in our coffee store, we will not make **roast** a field on the Compare Products page. However, if we later add an Attribute called **character**, that would probably be a good one for the **Compare Products** page.

12. The **Use in Layered Navigation** setting enables your customers to filter Products based on this Attribute. When this is enabled, your customer sees a filter on the left side of the page, where (s)he can select values for this Attribute. Magento will then display only Products that have a value for the Attribute that falls within the range selected by the customer.

In the following screenshot, notice that the customer has selected the Category **Electronics** from the Navigation Menu at the top of the page. Also, notice that the customer can filter the results by three Attributes on the lefthand side of the page. They are **Price**, **Color**, and **Manufacturer** as shown in the following screenshot:

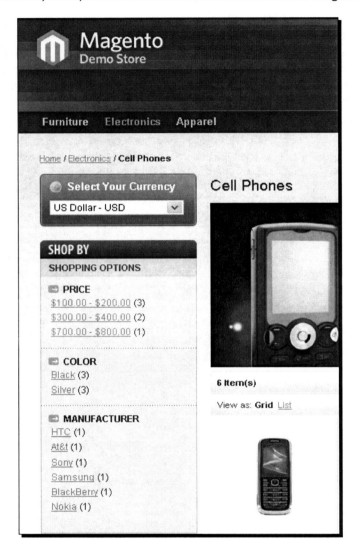

The customer can now find the Products that (s)he wants, using two criteria. A Category can be selected from the Navigation Menu at the top of the page. And, an Attribute Filter can be selected from the Layered Navigation menu on the left side of the page.

Notice the values for the Attribute **Price**. The first range covers $100 to $200. Then, the values jump to $300. The Price range $200 to $300 is missing. This is because no Products in this Category fall in that price range.

There are three settings for **Use in Layered Navigation**. Selecting **No** excludes this Attribute from the Layered Navigation menu.

Selecting **Filterable (with results)** will put the Attribute into the Layered Navigation menu, but only for those values that show some Products. That is, it places only those values that produce results when used as a filter. That is what happened in the previous screenshot.

Selecting **Filterable (no results)** will put the Attribute into the Layered Navigation menu, and all values will be displayed. Even values that don't produce results will be displayed. If that setting were selected in the page we just saw, the Price range $200-$300 would be displayed, even though there are no Products in that range.

You can make an attribute filterable only if the **Input Type** is **Dropdown**, **Multiple Select**, or **Price**.

13. If you use this Attribute in the Layered Navigation menu (that is, if you allow your customers to filter by this Attribute), then **Position** determines the position of the attribute in the Layered Navigation. Entering **1** puts this Attribute at the top of the menu.

14. The setting for **Visible on Catalog Pages on Front-end** applies only to Simple Attributes. That is, it applies only to Attributes that you create, not to those that are automatically created by Magento.

Every product page has a section called **Additional Information**. It displays below the **Product Description** section. In the following screenshot, you can see this section:

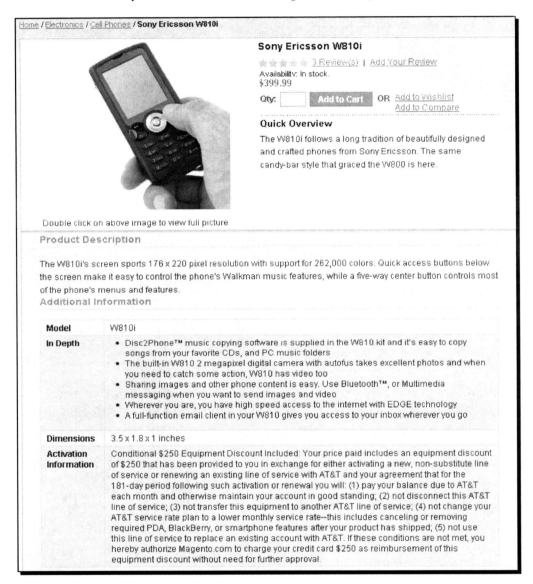

Home / Electronics / Cell Phones / **Sony Ericsson W810i**

Sony Ericsson W810i

★ ★ ★ ★ ★ 3 Review(s) | Add Your Review
Availability: In stock.
$399.99

Qty: [   ] **Add to Cart** OR Add to Wishlist
Add to Compare

Quick Overview

The W810i follows a long tradition of beautifully designed and crafted phones from Sony Ericsson. The same candy-bar style that graced the W800 is here.

Double click on above image to view full picture

Product Description

The W810i's screen sports 176 x 220 pixel resolution with support for 262,000 colors. Quick access buttons below the screen make it easy to control the phone's Walkman music features, while a five-way center button controls most of the phone's menus and features.

Additional Information

Model	W810i
In Depth	• Disc2Phone™ music copying software is supplied in the W810 kit and it's easy to copy songs from your favorite CDs, and PC music folders • The built-in W810 2 megapixel digital camera with autofus takes excellent photos and when you need to catch some action, W810 has video too • Sharing images and other phone content is easy. Use Bluetooth™, or Multimedia messaging when you want to send images and video • Wherever you are, you have high speed access to the internet with EDGE technology • A full-function email client in your W810 gives you access to your inbox wherever you go
Dimensions	3.5 x 1.8 x 1 inches
Activation Information	Conditional $250 Equipment Discount Included: Your price paid includes an equipment discount of $250 that has been provided to you in exchange for either activating a new, non-substitute line of service or renewing an existing line of service with AT&T and your agreement that for the 181-day period following such activation or renewal you will: (1) pay your balance due to AT&T each month and otherwise maintain your account in good standing; (2) not disconnect this AT&T line of service; (3) not transfer this equipment to another AT&T line of service; (4) not change your AT&T service rate plan to a lower monthly service rate--this includes canceling or removing required PDA, BlackBerry, or smartphone features after your product has shipped; (5) not use this line of service to replace an existing account with AT&T. If these conditions are not met, you hereby authorize Magento.com to charge your credit card $250 as reimbursement of this equipment discount without need for further approval.

If you select **Yes** for **Visible on Catalog Pages on Front-end**, this Attribute will appear in the **Additional Information** section of each Product that uses the Attribute. In the previous example, the Attributes Model, In Depth, Dimensions, and Activation Information had **Visible on Catalog Pages on Front-end** set to **Yes**.

If a Product has no Attributes that are **Visible on Catalog Pages on Front-end**, then the Additional Information section will not display for that Product.

15. Select the **Manage Labels/Options** tab:

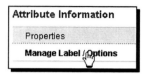

16. Under **Manage Titles** in the **Admin** field, enter the name that you will use for this Attribute in the administrative interface. In the **Default Store View** field enter the name for this Attribute that your customers will see in your store:

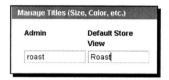

17. If this Attribute type is **Dropdown** or **Multiple Select**, then the **Manage Options** section will appear:

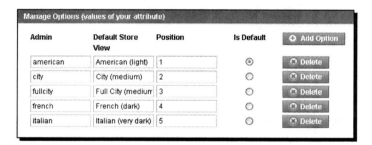

Recall that when an Attribute is a dropdown or multiple selection, you must select one or more values for that Attribute from a list. The **Manage Options** section is where you create that list.

In the **Admin** field, enter the name that you will use for this value in the administrative interface. You will see this name when you are creating a Product, and assigning a value to the Attribute. In the **Default Store View** field, enter the value that your customers will see in your store.

If this Attribute type is not **Dropdown** or **Multiple Select**, then this section will not appear.

18. Click on **Save Attribute**. The Attribute is saved and you are returned to the list of Attributes. You should see the one you just added in the list, along with a success message at the top of the page like this:

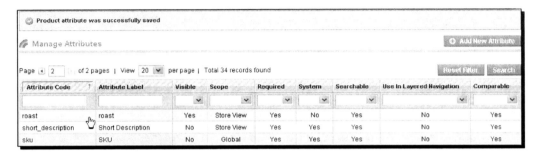

This concludes the process for creating a new Attribute. Repeat this as needed. In our demonstration store, we will create two more Attributes: **grind** and **caffeine**.

What just happened?

In this section you created new Attributes. These Attributes will be used to describe your Products. Your customers will be able to use some of these Attributes to filter Products, helping them to drill down to exactly the merchandise they want. Other Attributes will appear in the Search function, enabling your customers to search your entire site for Products that meet their criteria. Your customers will also be able to use some of these Attributes when they compare products side-by-side, helping them to choose between the Products.

What's next?

Next, we will put our Attributes into Attribute Sets. Recall that you do not apply Attributes individually to Products. Instead, you apply a set of Attributes to each Product.

Time for action: Creating Attribute Sets

1. If you haven't already, log in to your site's backend. We call it the Administrative Panel.

2. Select **Catalog | Attributes | Manage Attribute Sets**.

   The **Manage Attribute Sets** page is displayed. If this is a new installation, there will be only one Attribute set listed—**Default** as shown in the following screenshot:

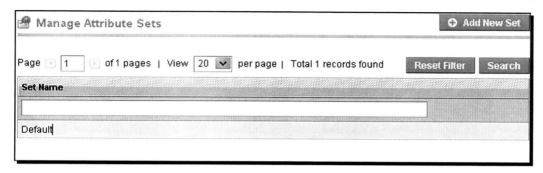

3. Click on **Add New Attribute Set**. The **Edit Set Name** page is displayed as follows:

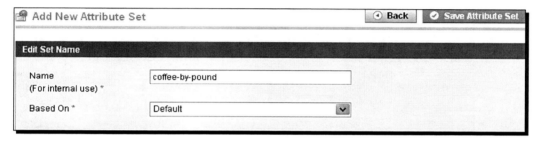

4. Enter a **Name** for this set. The shoppers will never see the name of this Attribute set. You will see the name when you create a Product and need to assign a set to that Product. This is why you should use a name that will help you remember the purpose of this set.

If you will use the set only for a specific kind of merchandise, consider naming the set after that merchandise. In the previous screenshot, I am creating a set that I will apply only to coffee sold by the pound. The name **coffee-by-pound** reminds me of the purpose for this set.

If you will apply this set to several kinds of merchandise, consider using a name that describes the contents of the set. In our demo site, we could create a set that contains those Attributes called grind-roast-origin.

5. For **Based On**, select a set that will be the starting point for this set. If this is the first set that you created, then your only choice will be **Default**.

When you create a new set, you must always base it upon an existing set. The first time, this will be Default because that is the only set available.

Default contains all of the system Attributes that are required for each Product, plus a few more Attributes that come with the standard Magento installation.

You can edit the contents of Default, but you should not do this without a compelling reason. Leaving Default intact ensures that you will always have a set that contains the minimum Attributes needed for a Product. When you need to create a set that is very different from any of the others in your store, it is usually easiest to start with a minimum set such as Default and build it up. This is easier than starting with another set, removing the Attributes that you have added, and then building it up. Starting with Default and building up is easier when making new sets that are unlike any others in your store.

6. Click on **Save Attribute Set**. The **Edit Attribute Set** window is displayed:

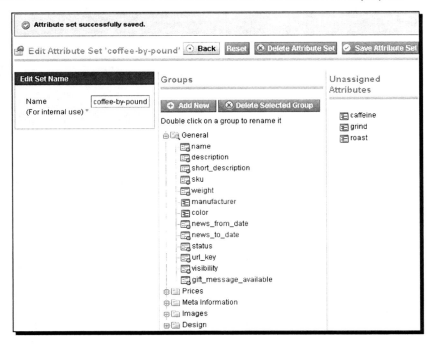

The left column contains the name of this set. The middle column contains all of the Attributes that are a part of this set. Right now, those are the same as for the Default set. The right column contains Attributes that are not part of this set. The label **Unassigned Attributes** might be misleading because these Attributes might have been assigned to other sets.

Notice that the Attributes in this set are organized into **Groups**. Each Group in this set will create a tab on the Product page if at least one Attribute in that Group is set to display. If all of the Attributes in a Group are hidden from the shopper, then that Group will not create a tab on the Product page. For example, the group Meta Information contains only Attributes that are hidden, so shoppers will not see a tab called Meta Information.

The orange circles mark the System Attributes. Recall that every set must contain all of the System Attributes because each Product must have all of the System Attributes applied to it.

7. To add an Attribute to the set, open a Group and then drag the Attribute into that Group as shown in the following screenshot:

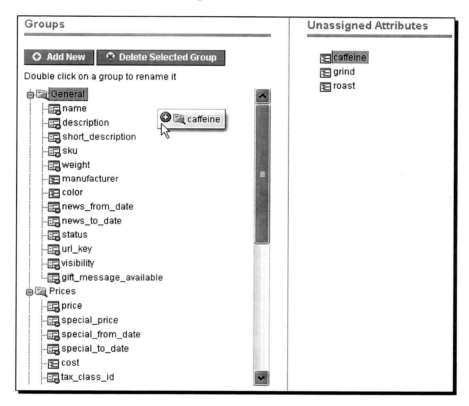

In our demo store, we will add **caffeine, grind,** and **roast** to the **General** group.

8. To remove an Attribute from the set, drag it from the Group that contains it to the **Unassigned Attributes** column.

In our demo store, we will remove **manufacturer** and **color** because they do not apply to our coffee product.

9. To move an Attribute from one Group to another Group, just drag and drop the Attribute.

10. To add a new Group (and possibly create a new tab on the Product page), click on **Add New**. When prompted, enter the name of the new Group.

11. To change the order of the Groups, drag and drop them.

The tabs that these Groups create on the Product page display left to right. They appear in the order that the Groups are placed here. The topmost Group creates the tab on the left, and the bottom Group creates the rightmost tab.

12. To delete a group, select it and click on **Delete Selected Group**.

You cannot delete a Group that has System Attributes in it. When you delete a Group, its Attributes become unassigned. When you are finished, click on **Save Attribute Set**.

What just happened?

You have just created at least one Attribute set. Each set contains a collection of Attributes that you will use to describe a product. If you created just one set, every Product in your site will use that set. This is fine if all your Products are similar (for example, if all you sell is coffee). If you created several sets, you probably sell several different kinds of Products (for example, coffee and coffee brewing accessories).

Pop quiz

1. The Layered Navigation Menu:
   - ❑ Displays all Categories in the store.
   - ❑ Displays only those Categories that are Anchors.
   - ❑ Displays Anchor Categories at the top level and subcategories beneath that.

2. Designating an Attribute as Filterable makes the Attribute appear:
   - ❑ In the Advanced Search page.
   - ❑ In the Layered Navigation menu.
   - ❑ On the Front Page.

For the answer, check out this screencast at the Magento web site: http://www.magentocommerce.com/media/screencasts/layerednavigation/view.

Summary

In this chapter, we created Categories that will hold our Products. Think of a Category as a department in a physical store. Then, we created Attributes and Attribute Sets. Think of Attributes as the qualities that enable us to distinguish one product from another.

In the next chapter, we will finish our basic set up by adding a Tax Class for our Products. Then, we will be ready to start adding Products.

4
Taxes

In the real world, the tax rate that you pay is based on three things: location, product type, and purchaser type. In Magento, we can create Tax Rules that determine the amount of tax that a customer pays, based upon the shipping address, product class, and customer class.

When you buy a product, you sometimes pay sales tax on that product. The sales tax that you pay is based on:

- ◆ **Where** you purchased the product from. Tax rules vary in different cities, states, and countries.

- ◆ The **type of product** that you purchased. For example, many places don't tax clothing purchases. And, some places tax only some kinds of clothing. This means that you must be able to apply different tax rates to different kinds of products.

- ◆ The **type of purchaser** you are. For example, if you buy a laser printer for your home, it is likely that you will pay sales tax. This is because you are a retail customer. If you buy the same printer for your business, in most places you will not pay sales tax. This is because you are a business customer.

- ◆ The **amount** of the purchase. For example, some places tax clothing purchases only above a specific amount.

Anatomy of a Tax Rule

A Tax Rule is a combination of the tax rate, shipping address, product class, customer class, and amount of purchase.

A Tax Rule states that you pay this amount of tax if you are this class of purchaser, and you bought this class of product for this amount, and are shipping it to this place.

The components of a Tax Rule are shown in the following screenshot. This screen is found under **Sales | Tax | Manage Tax Rules | Add New Tax Rule**.

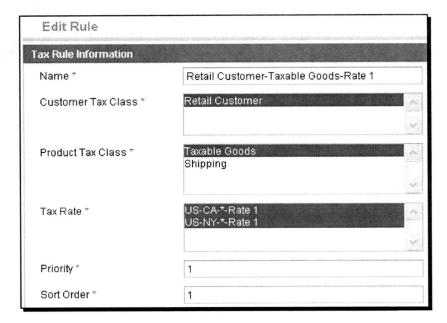

You will see the **Name** of the Tax Rule while working in the backend.

Customer Tax Class

Customer Tax Class is a type of customer that is making a purchase. Before creating a Tax Rule, you will need to have at least one Customer Tax Class. Magento provides you with a Tax Rule called Retail Customer. If you serve different types of customers—retail, business, and nonprofit—you will need to create different Customer Tax Classes.

Product Tax Class

Product Tax Class is a type of Product that is being purchased. When you create a Product, you will assign a Product Tax Class to that Product. Magento comes with two Product Tax Classes:Taxable Goods and Shipping. The class Shipping is applied to shipping charges because some places charge sales tax on shipping. If your customer's sales tax is different for different types of Products, then you will need to create a Product Tax Class for each type of Product.

Tax Rate

Tax Rate is a combination of place, or tax **zone**, and percentage. A zone can be a country, state, or zip code.

Each zone that you specify can have up to five sales tax percentages. For example, in the default installation of Magento, there is one tax rate for the zone **New York**. This is **8.3750** percent, and applies to retail customers. The following window can be found at **Sales | Tax | Manage Tax Zones & Rates** and then clicking on **US-NY-*-Rate 1**:

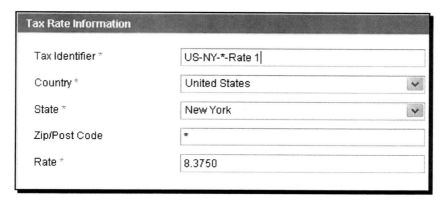

So in the screenshot of our Tax Rule, the Tax Rate **US-NY-*-Rate 1** doesn't mean "a sales tax of 1 percent." It means "Tax rate number 1 for **New York**, which is **8.3750** percent."

In this scenario, **New York** charges **8.3750** percent sales tax on retail sales. If New York does not charge sales tax for wholesale customers, and you sell to wholesale customers, then you will need to create another Tax Rate for New York:

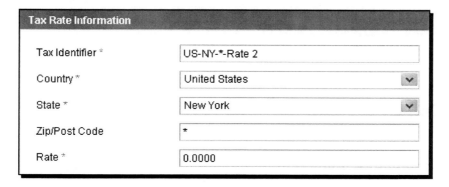

Whenever a zone has different sales taxes for different types of products or customers, you will need to create different Tax Rates for that zone.

Priority

If several Tax Rules try to apply several Tax Rates at the same time, how should Magento handle them? Should it add them all together? Or, should it apply one rate, calculate the total, and then apply the second rate to that total? That is, should Magento add them or compound them?

For example, suppose you sell a product in Philadelphia, Pennsylvania. Further suppose that according to the Tax Rule for Pennsylvania, the sales tax for that item is 6 percent, and that the Tax Rule for Philadelphia adds another 1 percent. In this case, you want Magento to add the two sales taxes. So, you would give the two Tax Rates the same Priority.

By contrast, Tax Rates that belong to Tax Rules with different Priorities are compounded. The Tax Rate with the higher Priority (the lower number) is applied, and the next higher Priority is applied to that total, and so on.

Sort Order

Sort Order determines the Tax Rules' position in the list of Tax Rules.

Why create Tax Rules now?

Why create a Tax Rule now, before adding our first Product? When you add a Product to your store, you put that Product into a Category, assign an Attribute Set, and select a Tax Class for that Product. By default, Magento comes with two Product Tax Classes and one Tax Rule already created. The Product Tax Classes are Taxable Goods and Shipping. The Tax Rule is **Retail Customer-Taxable Goods-Rate 1**. If you sell anything other than taxable goods, or sell to anyone other than retail customers, you will need to create a new Tax Rule to cover that situation.

Creating a Tax Rule

The process for creating a Tax Rule is:

1. Create the Customer Tax Classes that you need, or confirm that you have them.
2. Create the Product Tax Classes that you need, or confirm that you have them.
3. Create the Tax Rates that you need, or confirm that you have them and that they apply to the zones that you need.

4. Create and name the Tax Rule:

      ❏ Assign Customer Tax Class, Product Tax Class, and Tax Rates to the Rule.

      ❏ Use the Priority to determine whether the Rule is added, or compounded, with other Rules.

      ❏ Determine the Sort Order of the Rule and save it.

Each of these steps is covered in the subsections that follow.

Time for action: Creating a Customer Tax Class

1. From the Admin Panel, select **Sales | Tax | Customer Tax Classes**.

The **Customer Tax Classes** page is displayed. If this is a new installation, only one Class is listed, **Retail Customer** as shown in the following screenshot:

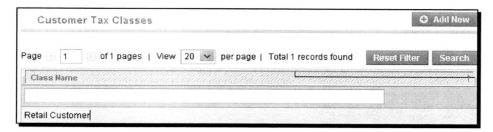

2. Click on **Add New**. A **Customer Tax Class Information** page is displayed.

3. Enter a name for the Customer Tax Class.

4. In our demo store, we are going to create Customer Tax Classes for Business and Nonprofit customers.

5. Click on **Save Class**. Repeat these steps until all of the Customer Tax Classes that you need have been created.

What just happened?

A Tax Rule is composed of a Customer Class, Product Class, Tax Rate, and the location of the purchaser. You have just created the first part of that formula: the Customer Class.

Time for action: Creating a Product Tax Class

1. From the Admin Panel, select **Sales | Tax | Product Tax Classes**.

   The Product Tax Classes page is displayed. If this is a new installation, only two Classes are listed: **Shipping** and **Taxable Goods**.

2. Click on **Add New**. The **Product Tax Class Information** page gets displayed:

   Product Tax Class Information

   Class Name *

3. Enter a name for the Product Tax Class.

   In our demo store, we are going to create Product Tax Classes for **Food** and **Nonfood** products. We will apply the **Food** class to the coffee that we sell. We will apply the **Nonfood** class to the mugs, coffee presses, and other coffee accessories that we sell.

4. Click on **Save Class**. Repeat these steps until all of the Product Tax Classes that you need have been created.

What just happened?

A Tax Rule is composed of a Customer Class, Product Class, Tax Rate, and the location of the purchaser. You have just created the second part of that formula: the Product Class.

Creating Tax Rates

In Magento, you can create Tax Rates one at a time. You can also import Tax Rates in bulk. Each method is covered in the next section.

Time for action: Creating a Tax Rate in Magento

1. From the Admin Panel, select **Sales | Tax | Manage Tax Zones & Rates**.

   The **Manage Tax Rates** page is displayed. If this is a new installation, only two Tax Rates are listed: **US-CA-*-Rate 1** and **US-NY-*-Rate 1**.

2. Click on **Add New Tax Rate**. The **Add New Tax Rate** page gets displayed:

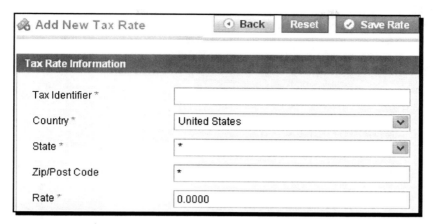

3. **Tax Identifier** is the name that you give this Tax Rate. You will see this name when you select this Tax Rate.

The example that we saw is named **US-CA-*-Rate 1**. Notice how this name tells you the **Country**, **State**, and **Zip/Post** code for the Tax Rate. (The asterisk indicates that it applies to all zip codes in California.) It also tells which rate applies. Notice that the name doesn't give the actual percentage, which is 8.25%. Instead, it says Rate 1. This is because the percentage can change when California changes its tax rate. If you include the actual rate in the name, you would need to rename this Tax Rate when California changes the rate. Another way this rate could have been named is US-CA-All-Retail. Before creating new Tax Rates, you should develop a naming scheme that works for you and your business.

4. **Country**, **State**, and **Zip/Post Code** determine the zone to which this Tax Rate applies. Magento calculates sales tax based upon the billing address, and not the shipping address. **Country** and **State** are drop-down lists. You must select from the options given to you. **Zip/Post Code** accepts both numbers and letters. You can enter an asterisk in this field and it will be a wild card. That is, the rate will apply to all zip/post codes in the selected country and state.

You can enter a zip/post code without entering a country or state. If you do this, you should be sure that zip/post code is unique in the entire world.

Suppose you have one tax rate for all zip codes in a country/state, such as 6% for United States/Pennsylvania. Also, suppose that you want to have a different tax rate for a few zip codes in that state. In this case, you would create separate tax rates for those few zip codes. The rates for the specific zip codes would override the rates for the wild card. So in a Tax Rate, a wild card means, "All zones unless this is overridden by a specific zone." In our demo store, we are going to create a Tax Rate for retail customers who live in the state of Pennsylvania, but not in the city of Philadelphia as shown:

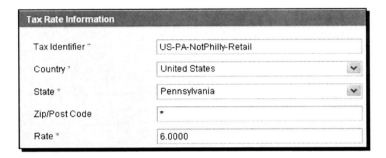

5. Click on **Save Rate**. You are taken back to the **Manage Tax Rates** page. The Tax Rate that you just added should be listed on the page.

This procedure is useful for adding Tax Rates one at a time. However, if you need to add many Tax Rates at once, you will probably want to use the Import Tax Rates feature. This enables you to import a `.csv`, or a text-only file. You usually create the file in a spreadsheet such as OpenOffice Calc or Excel. The next section covers importing Tax Rates.

What just happened?

A Tax Rule is composed of a Customer Class, Product Class, Tax Rate, and the location of the purchaser. You have just created the third part of that formula: the Tax Rate. The Tax Rate included the location and the percentage of tax. You created the Tax Rate by manually entering the information into the system, which is suitable if you don't have too many Tax Rates to type.

Time for action: Exporting and importing Tax Rates

In my demo store, I have created a Tax Rate for the state of Pennsylvania. The Tax Rate for the city of Philadelphia is different. However, Magento doesn't enable me to choose a separate Tax Rate based on the city. So I must create a Tax Rate for each zip code in the city of Philadelphia. At this time there are 84 zip codes, and are shown here:

19019	19092	19093	19099	19101	19102	19103	19104	19105	19106	19107
19108	19109	19110	19111	19112	19113	19114	19115	19116	19118	19119
19120	19121	19122	19123	19124	19125	19126	19127	19128	19129	19130
19131	19132	19133	19134	19135	19136	19137	19138	19139	19140	19141
19142	19143	19144	19145	19146	19147	19148	19149	19150	19151	19152
19153	19154	19155	19160	19161	19162	19170	19171	19172	19173	19175
19177	19178	19179	19181	19182	19183	19184	19185	19187	19188	19191
19192	19193	19194	19196	19197	19244	19255				

I don't want to manually create each of these Tax Rates in Magento. It would be much faster if I create them in a spreadsheet program, and import the file into Magento. The process will be like this:

1. Export the existing Tax Rates from Magento to a `.csv` (text-only) file.
2. Add the new Tax Rates and/or edit the existing ones.
3. Check the file in a text editor and convert to UNIX format.
4. Import the file and check that Magento has updated the Tax Rates.

Exporting Tax Rates

1. On the **Manage Tax Rates** page, select **CSV** from the **Export** drop-down menu as shown:

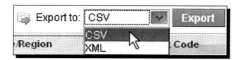

2. Click on **Export**.

3. You will be prompted to save or open the exported file. Choose the option that enables you to open the file in your spreadsheet application.

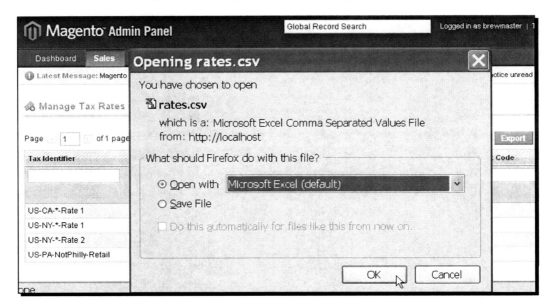

4. Now that the file is open in your spreadsheet, you can see the column headings in the first row and the Tax Rates in the rows below that:

	A	B	C	D	E	F
1	Code	Country	State	Zip/Post Code	Rate	default
2	US-CA-*-Rate 1	US	CA	*	8.25	
3	US-NY-*-Rate 1	US	NY	*	8.375	
4	US-NY-*-Rate 2	US	NY	*	0	
5	US-PA-NotPhilly-Retail	US	PA	*	6	

Adding the new Tax Rates and/or editing the existing ones

1. Edit the spreadsheet as needed. In our demo store, we collect sales tax only in Pennsylvania. So, we will delete the rows for CA and NY.

2. Adding the 84 zip codes for Philadelphia is as simple as pasting them into the spreadsheet. The result is 84 new rows:

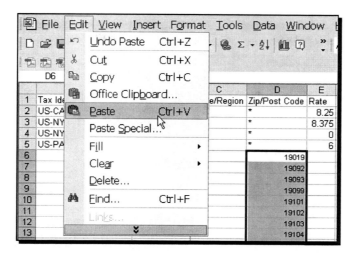

3. Now fill in the **Country** and **State/Region** columns. In most spreadsheets, you can enter the values into the first row, select the first cell and the ones below that, and fill the lower cells with the contents of the top cell:

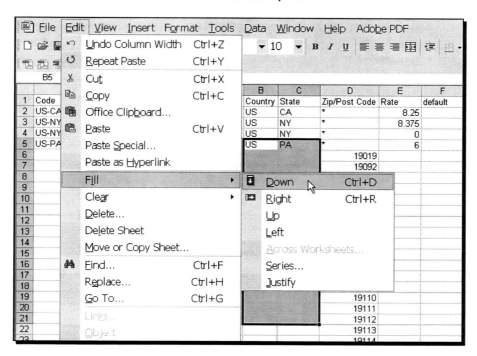

4. You probably want the name of the Tax Rate to use the same format as the others, **Country-State-ZipCode-TypeOfRate**. For example, the first rate for Philadelphia would be called **US-PA-Philly-19019-Retail**. However, I do not want to type all of the 84 names. So, I will use the CONCATENATE function in my spreadsheet to join the different parts of the name into one text string as shown in the following screenshot:

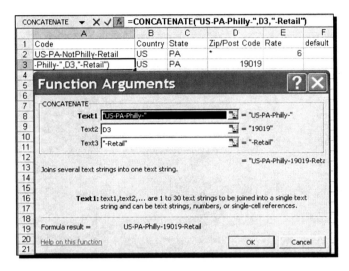

5. Notice that the first part of the name consists of the text **US-PA-Philly-**. Then, this function looks at the cell in column D, which is the zip code. Finally, it adds the text**–Retail** to the end of the text string. The result is the name of the Tax Rate.

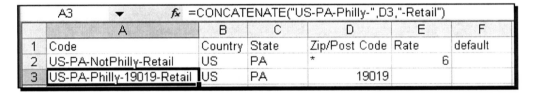

Finally, use **Fill | Down** to copy this formula into the other 83 rows.

6. Save the spreadsheet as a `.csv`, or text-only, file. Make a note of where you save it.

Checking the file in a text editor and converting it to a UNIX format

When using a text file, Magento may display an error reading **Invalid file format upload attempt**, your text file is probably saved in a Windows or Macintosh, text-only format. Even though text-only files look the same on Windows, Mac, and UNIX (Linux), they are not. Before Magento can read the file, you need to convert the file to the UNIX format.

We need to use a text editor designed to work with Windows/Mac/UNIX formats. On Windows, try the free program TedNPad. On Mac, try TextWrangler. Now, let's convert it to a UNIX format:

1. Open the file using a text-editing program. Make sure your spreadsheet saved the file in the correct format.

   Here are the first few lines of my `.csv` file:

   ```
   "Code","Country","State","Zip/Post Code","Rate","default"
   "US-PA-NotPhilly-Retail","US","PA","*","6.0000",""
   "US-PA-Philly-19019-Retail","US","PA","19019","7.0000",""
   "US-PA-Philly-19092-Retail","US","PA","19092","7.0000",""
   "US-PA-Philly-19093-Retail","US","PA","19093","7.0000",""
   ```

   Notice that each item of data is enclosed in double quotes. Also, notice that each tax rate has four decimal places.

2. In your text editor, save the file in the UNIX format. For example, in TedNPad you select **File | Save in Unix** as shown:

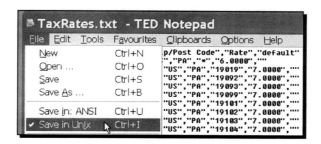

   Notice that I've named the file `TaxRates.txt`. The filename extension really doesn't matter, as long as the file is text-only, saved in the UNIX format, and follows the format that we saw.

Importing the file and checking that Magento has updated the Tax Rates

1. In Magento, select **Sales | Tax | Import/Export Tax Rates**.

2. Click on the **Browse...** button and select the file that you created.

3. After selecting the file, click on **Import Tax Rates**.

4. When the file is finished importing, you should see a message stating **Tax rate was successfully imported**.

5. Select **Sales | Tax | Manage Tax Zones & Rates** and check the list of Tax Rates to ensure that yours were imported.

What just happened?

A Tax Rule is composed of a Customer Class, Product Class, Tax Rate, and the location of the purchaser. We have just created the third part of that formula: the Tax Rates. Each Tax Rate included the location and the percentage of tax. We created these Tax Rates by exporting a template from Magento. We opened this template in Excel, entered the tax rates, and saved it as a text file. Finally, we imported the Tax Rates back into Magento.

Time for action: Creating a Tax Rule

Finally, after creating the Customer Tax Classes, Product Tax Classes, and Tax Rates/Zones that we need, we are ready to create Tax Rules. For our demo store, we will need only one Tax Rule.

Retail customers who purchase non-food items within Pennsylvania (including Philadelphia) pay sales tax.

All other purchases are tax-free, so we don't need any Tax Rules to cover them.

1. Go to **Sales | Tax | Manage Tax Rules**.

The **Manage Tax Rules** page is displayed.

2. Click on **Add New Tax Rule**. The **New Rule** page is displayed.

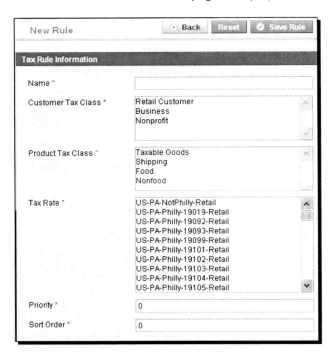

Notice that all of the Customer Tax Classes, Product Tax Classes, and Tax Rates/Zones that you created are displayed here. The Tax Rule will be a combination of these three elements. You can choose one or more of each element.

3. Enter a **Name** for the Tax Rule.

In our demo store, we want the name to indicate the purpose of the Rule. So we will enter a name that tells us the type of customer, product, and rate/zone the Rule contains.

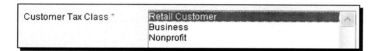

4. Select one or more **Customer Tax Classes** for the Rule.

In our demo store, we want this rule to apply only to **Retail Customer**s.

5. Select one or more **Product Tax Classes** for the Rule.

In our demo store, we want this rule to apply only to **Nonfood** items.

6. Select one or more **Tax Rates** for the Rule.

In our demo store, we want this rule to apply to all zones in **PA**.

7. Click on **Save Rule**.

8. You are returned to the **Manage Tax Rules** page. You should see the Rule that you just added listed there, as seen in the following screenshot:

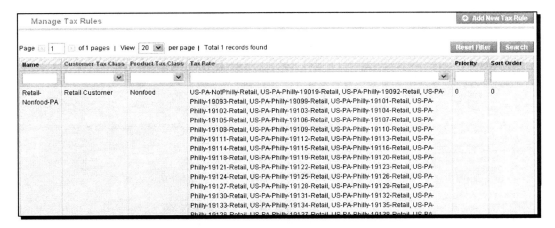

What just happened?

A Tax Rule is composed of a Customer Class, Product Class, Tax Rate, and the location of the purchaser. You have just combined these elements into a Tax Rule. This Rule will apply to the unique combination of customer/product/location.

Pop quiz

1. Choose the three elements that combine to form a Tax Rule:

   a.   Customer class

   b.   Product class

   c.   Tax rate

   d.   Location

2. When you use a spreadsheet to create Tax Rules, what must you do in Magento before adding those Rules to the spreadsheet?

   a.   Export a template.

   b.   Create the locations.

   c.   Type in the rates.

Summary

In this chapter, we saw how a Tax Rule combines the zone/rate, product type, and purchaser type into a Rule that determines the tax on a product. We created these components first, and then combined them into a Rule.

Now that we have created Categories, Attributes, and Tax Rules, we are ready to add Products to our store.

5

Adding Simple Products

In Magento, you can add a Simple Product, a Grouped Product, or a Configurable Product. Until you have added several Simple Products, the other two choices don't make much sense.

The following is the procedure for adding a simple product, which is divided into seven parts.

Part 1: Adding the Product and assigning an Attribute Set

In this part of the process, you will create the blank Product and select an Attribute Set for the Product. The Attribute Set will determine which Attributes are available for the Product.

 Once you have assigned an Attribute Set to a Product, you cannot remove that Set and apply a different one.

The Product now permanently uses that Attribute Set. You can edit the Set under **Catalog | Attributes**. This will change the Attributes in the Set and, therefore, the Attributes that the Product has. However, you cannot remove the Set from the Product.

Time for action: Creating the Product and selecting an Attribute Set

1. Log in to your site's backend, which we call the Administrative Panel.

2. Select **Catalog | Manage Products** as shown:

The **Manage Products** page is displayed. Because you haven't added any products yet, the list of products is blank as shown in the following screenshot:

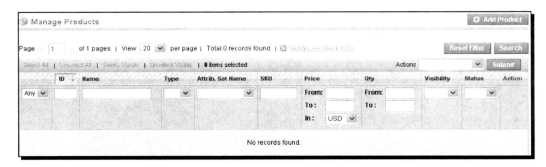

3. Click on **Add Product**. The **Create Product Settings** page is displayed.

4. Select an **Attribute Set**.

> If you don't know what an Attribute Set is, stop here and read Chapter 3 before proceeding.

In our demo store, we will use the Attribute Set **coffee-by-pound**, which we created in the previous chapter.

> Once you assign an Attribute Set to a Product and select its Product Type, these cannot be changed. Therefore, make sure that before you create a Product, you have chosen the correct Product Type, and you have created the Attribute Set that you want to use.

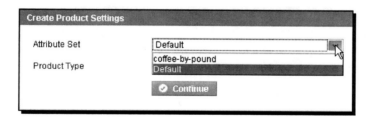

5. Leave **Product Type** set to **Simple Product**. Until you have added several Simple Products, the other two choices (**Grouped Product** and **Configurable Product**) don't make much sense.

6. Click on **Continue**. The **Product Information** page is displayed as shown in the following screenshot:

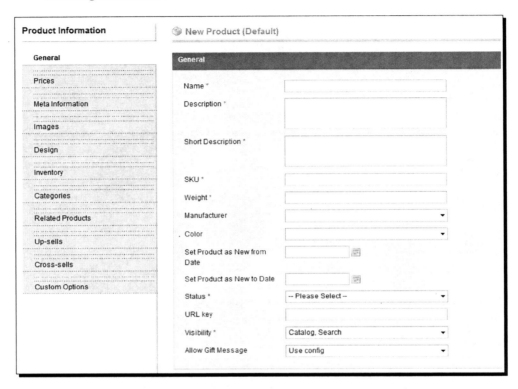

This page is divided into tabs, which you see listed on the left side. We won't discuss all of the fields in all of the tabs. Instead, we'll cover the fields and tabs that you are most likely to use when you are first creating your store.

The **General** tab is selected for you. Let's begin there.

What just happened?

We just created a new, blank Simple Product. This is the most basic type of Product in Magento. We assigned an Attribute Set to that Product, which gives it a list of Attributes. The rest of this process will mostly consist of entering values for those Attributes.

Part 2: The General tab

When Magento displays a product in your store, that product appears on its own page. Most of the information that your shoppers see on that page is entered in the **General** tab:

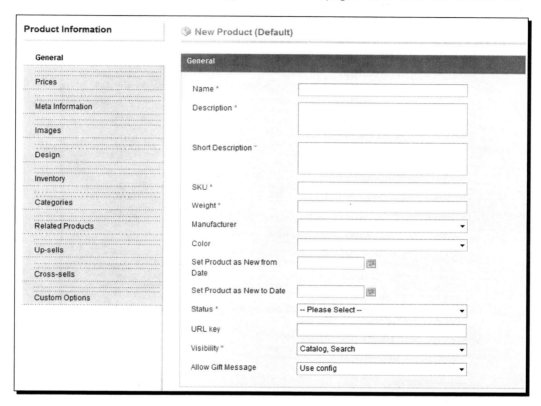

Notice that several fields on this page are marked with red asterisks. These fields are required, so you must fill them. There is also a required field under the **Prices** tab.

 You must fill in the required fields under the **General** and **Prices** tabs before leaving the **New Product** page. Even if you save your work, the product will not be added to your store if you haven't filled in the required fields.

Time for action: Filling the fields on the General tab

Each of the fields in the **General** tab is described next. Fill in the fields for your Product.

1. **Name, Description, and Short Description**

Your customers will see the product **Name** at the top of the product's page. A **Short Description** appears below it, and a **Description** below it.

When shoppers **List** the products in a Category, they also see the **Name** and **Short Description** as shown in the following screenshot:

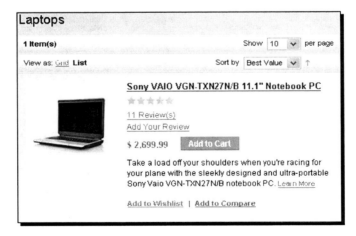

2. SKU

SKU stands for **Stock Keeping Unit**. This is a standard term in the retail industry. Each item in your store must have a unique SKU. For more about SKUs, see the Wikipedia article at `http://es.wikipedia.org/wiki/Stock_Keeping_Unit`.

3. Weight

This field is the product's weight. Usually, this field holds the **shipping weight**, and not the **actual** weight of the product. You usually put the actual weight of the product in the product's description. You usually use this field for calculating the cost of shipping.

For example, the **Product Description** for the laptop states that it weighs 2.84 pounds. However, the shipping weight would be much higher because it includes the box, accessories, packaging, and manuals.

Our coffee store is an exception because we sell products by weight. So, we will take the unusual step of using the **Weight** field for the product's actual weight.

Most of our coffee will be sold in one-pound bags. However, if we want to offer a half-pound or two-pound bag, we'll need to create separate products for each of them.

4. **Set Product as New from Date** and **Set Product as New to Date**

The default layout for Magento's home page shows blocks that display the shopper's recently viewed products, and products that the shopper chooses to compare. You can also add some code to your store's home page that will display new products. The new products will appear at the bottom of the page. Magento can also put new products into an RSS feed and send email announcements of new products, for customers who subscribe.

A new product can be included in the new product display, RSS feed, and/or email announcement.

Setting dates in the fields for **Set Product as New from/to Date** makes the product "new" to Magento. If you use any of the above features, you will need to fill in these date fields. However, if you don't highlight "new" products in your store, you can safely leave these fields blank.

5. **Status**

Enabled makes this product active and displays it in your store. **Disabled** makes this product inactive and hides it from shoppers. I prefer to keep a product **Disabled** until I've filled out all the tabs, and double-checked my work.

6. **URL key**

Some features can cause a web page to rank higher in search engines. Designing a page to appear as high as possible in search engines is called **search engine optimization**, or **SEO**. It is part science and part art. A full discussion is beyond the scope of this chapter.

One feature that helps a page's search engine rank is a URL that has relevant search terms in it. For example, `brew-me-a-cup.com/product/1234` is not a search engine friendly URL. However, `brew-me-a-cup.com/kona-fancy-wholebean` gives a search engine more information to index.

The **URL key** field creates a search engine friendly URL. Because a URL cannot have spaces or special characters; you cannot use them in this field. If you leave this field blank, Magento will generate a search engine friendly URL for you. It will base this URL on the product's **Name**.

7. **Visibility**

This field determines whether the product will not display at all in your site (**Nowhere**), display on the pages of your site (**Catalog**), show up in search results (**Search**), or both (**Catalog, Search**). Note that even if a product's **Status** is set to **Enabled**, you must have its **Visibility** set to **Catalog** or **Search**, or your shoppers won't be able to see or find it. If you have the **Status** set to **Disabled**, then the Product won't show up in the Catalog no matter what you've set the **Visibility** to. However, you can set **Visibility** to **Search** for a Disabled product.

8. **Allow Gift Message**

This field determines if customers can add a gift message to this product during checkout. **Yes** and **No** are self-explanatory. **Use config** means that for this product, Magento will use the sitewide setting for gift messages. You will find that setting under **System | Sales | Sales | Gift Messages**.

9. **Save** and Continue to Pricing

In the upper right corner of the **New Product** page, there are two buttons:

Save will save what you have entered into this tab, and advance you to the next tab. **Save and Continue Edit** will save the information that you entered and keep you on the same tab. Because there is a required field on the next tab, you will want to **Save** this tab and proceed to the **Prices** tab. This is because you must fill in all required fields before the system will allow you to save the product.

What just happened?

Now that you have filled in values for the Attributes on the **General** tab, you are halfway in completing the minimum information for this Product.

You have a few fields under **Prices** to fill out. Then, it's on to the optional information under the rest of the tabs.

Part 3: The Prices tab

Under the **Prices** tab, you enter all of the pricing information for the product. This includes:

- The normal **Price**
- A **Special Price**
- Your **Cost** for the product

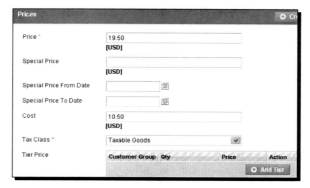

Time for action: Entering pricing for the Product

Each of the fields under the **Prices** tab is described in the following subsections—fill in the required fields plus any optional fields that you want to use:

1. **Special Price**

   If you enter a **Special Price**, the original **Price** will be displayed with a red line through it, and the Special Price will be displayed. If you do not enter any dates, the **Special Price** will be in effect until you remove it. If you do enter dates, the **Special Price** will be in effect during the dates specified.

   This is not the only place where you can determine the price of a product. You can also use an advanced feature called a Shopping Cart Price Rule. This rule can change the price of a product based on what other products are in the Shopping Cart. A **Shopping Cart Price Rule** takes effect in the Shopping Cart during the checkout process so that customers don't see them until they've added the Product to their carts. A **Special Price** is displayed on the catalog page so customers see it before they add the Product to their carts.

2. **Tax Class**

   The **Tax Class** that you select here determines how the product gets taxed.

    If you don't know what a Tax Class and a Tax Rule are, stop here and read Chapter 4 before proceeding.

   In our demo store, we will give this Product a **Tax Class** of **Food**.

3. **Tier Pricing**

   Tier Pricing enables you to give different prices for different quantities. Usually, you use this to give a discount for buying in bulk. You can apply tiered pricing to all, or to certain groups of customers.

   There is more about Tiered Pricing in Chapter 7.

What just happened?

Your product now contains pricing information. You have completed all of the mandatory information for a product. Now, it's on to the optional information under the rest of the tabs.

Part 4: The Meta Information tab

The **Meta Keywords** and **Meta Description** appear under meta tags, in the page's HTML code. Enter information about this Product that you think will help search engines to properly categorize this page.

A meta tag contains information not normally displayed to the user. The word meta means *about this subject* and the meta tags contain information about the page. Webmasters use meta tags to tell search engines about a page, and to help search engines better categorize that page.

You can see the meta tags in a page if you view the pages' source code.

Time for action: Entering Meta information

1. For **Meta Title**, enter the title for this Product page. The keywords should be search terms that customers will use when searching for this kind of a product.

2. For **Meta Keywords**, enter keywords that describe this Product. The keywords should be search terms that customers will use when searching for this kind of product.

3. For **Meta Description**, enter a single sentence, or phrase, that describes the Product. If a potential customer found this Product on a search site such as Google or Teoma, what description would you like the customer to see? That is what you should enter here.

What just happened?

You have used **Meta Keywords** and **Meta Description** as opportunities to optimize the Product's page for search engines.

Part 5: The Images tab

By default, Magento uses three images for each Product: base, small, and thumbnail. The base image is displayed on the Product's home page. The small image is displayed when a Product appears in a list of other Products, such as when you are viewing a Category landing page. The thumbnail image appears in the Shopping Cart, and in blocks that show recently added items and other items that the customer may be interested in.

Before you upload: Resizing images

The default stylesheet in Magento usually displays thumbnail images at 50-by-50 or 75-by-75 pixels. Small images are usually displayed at 125-by-125 or 135-by-135 pixels. Base images are usually displayed at 265-by-265 pixels. You can upload any size image, and Magento will resize it when displaying the image. However, there are some advantages to sizing the images yourself.

First, while Magento does a good job of resizing the images, it is not a graphic editing application. Some images will look better if you resize them with a specialized graphic editing software such as PhotoShop or GIMP. If you want to be sure of the resized image's quality, do it yourself instead of depending upon Magento.

Second, resizing an image yourself enables you to preview the image at the final display size. For example, suppose you upload the following image for one of your Products:

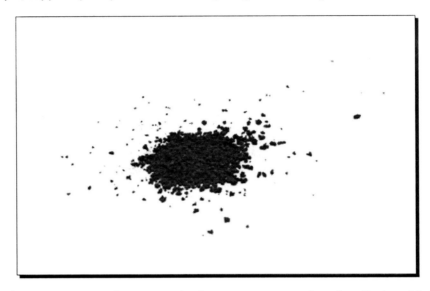

The size of this image is 400-by-267 pixels. On a computer monitor that displays 96 dots per inch, the image would be about 4.2-by-2.8 inches. At this size, you can see that it is a pile of grounded coffee. However, if you let Magento resize this image to 75-by-75 pixels, it becomes unrecognizable.

Instead of depending upon Magento to resize the image, let's crop and resize it ourselves. It now looks as follows:

Remember that the base image is displayed on the Product's home page. If the base image that you upload is larger than 265-by-265 pixels, shoppers will be able to zoom in and see more detail.

To summarize, before uploading images for your Product, you should at least crop the images to fill the space with as much Product as possible. For a thumbnail image, crop the image so that the subject will be recognizable at 75-by-75 pixels, or about three quarters of an inch square. Magento will resize images for you. However, if you want to be sure about how they will look at various sizes, resize the images in a graphics program before you upload them.

Time for action: Uploading images

After you have created your Product images, it is time to upload them. The following are the steps to upload your images:

1. On the **Product Information** page, select the **Images** tab.
2. Click on **Browse Files...**; a dialog box appears, where you select one file for uploading.

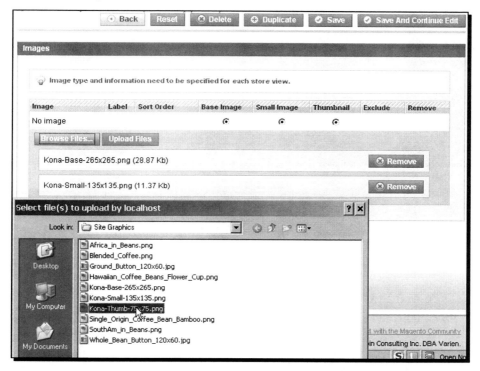

3. Select an image to upload, and then click on the **Open** or **OK** button in the dialog box.
4. If you want the same image to be used for the base, small, and thumbnail images, you can move to the next step. If you want to use separate images for all the three images, then click on **Browse Files...** and select more images.

5. After you select all the images that you want for this Product, click on **Upload Files**. The files will be uploaded to the images page as shown in the following screenshot:

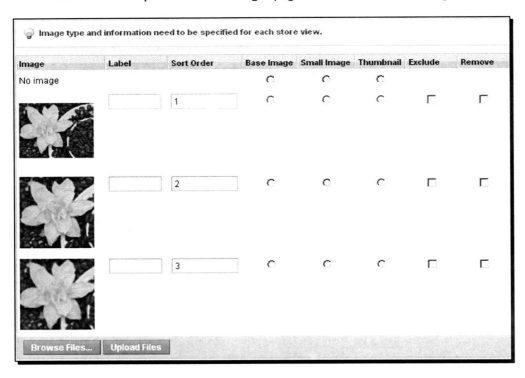

6. Select the image that you want for **Base Image**, **Small Image**, and **Thumbnail** by clicking the radio buttons, which can be seen in the following screenshot:

7. To exclude an image type, click on the radio button in the top row for **No Image**. This means that wherever Magento would have used that image size, no image will be displayed. For example, the thumbnail image appears in the Shopping Cart. If you select **No Image** for the **Thumbnail** image, then no image will be added when this is placed in the Shopping Cart. You might use **No Image** when you are selling something for which an image doesn't make sense. For example, if you're selling a repair service you might not need an image.

8. Enter a **Label** for each image. This will be used as the "alt text" for that image.

9. Click on **Save And Continue Edit**.

What just happened?

You should now have at least one image, and possibly several more, for your Product. Each image should be optimized for the size at which it will display. You have also entered the alt text for each image.

The **Design** tab is next on the menu. We will skip that tab because it is beyond the scope of a beginner's guide. Instead, let's proceed to the **Inventory** tab.

Part 6: The Inventory tab

Notice that all of the settings on the **Inventory** tab, except for **Qty** and **Stock Availability**, use the global configuration as shown:

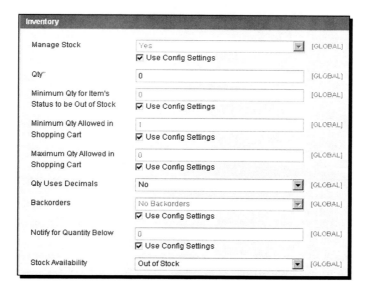

You will find these global inventory settings under **System | Configuration | Catalog | Inventory**. Look at the following screenshot:

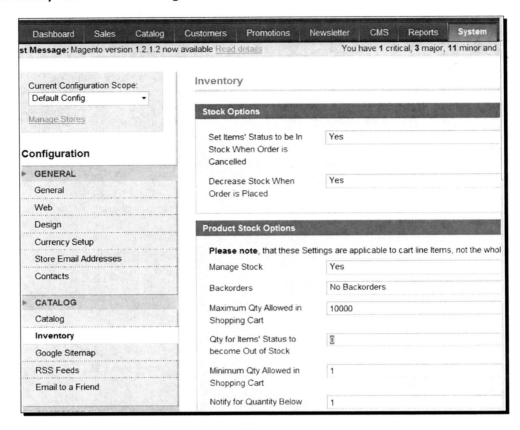

Let's return to the Product's **Inventory** tab and examine each of these fields. Remember that except for **Qty** and **Stock Availability**, each of these fields is found on both the Product and system configuration pages. Choose the one you want to edit (the Product or the Global settings) and navigate to that page. Next, select a setting for each of the following fields. The following table shows the settings that we used for our demo store:

Field	Appears in Catalog | Manage Products | Product | Inventory	Appears in System | Configuration | Catalog | Inventory	Explanation
Manage Stock	✓	✓	If this is set to **Yes**, then by default Magento will keep track of inventory for a Product. If it's set to **No**, then Magento will not keep track of inventory and all the other settings are irrelevant for the Product. The individual setting for the Product overrides the setting for the System.
Qty	✓		This is the quantity that you have in stock.
Set Items' Status to be In Stock When Order is Cancelled		✓	This will "return" items to stock when an order with that item is cancelled. Otherwise, you must manually return the item to stock by adding it to the quantity field.
Decrease Stock When Order is Placed		✓	This global setting makes Magento automatically deduct items from the quantity when those items are ordered.
Backorders	✓	✓	This setting determines if you allow customers to backorder an item that is out of stock.
Maximum Qty Allowed in Shopping Cart	✓	✓	The maximum quantity allowed in one order.
Qty for Items' Status to become Out of Stock	✓	✓	If the number in stock falls below this threshold, it is shown as Out of Stock. If you run both an online and physical store, you might want to keep a few items on the shelf, so you would set this to some number above zero.
Minimum Qty Allowed in Shopping Cart	✓	✓	The minimum quantity allowed in one order.
Notify for Quantity Below	✓	✓	When the quantity in stock drops below this number, Magento emails the store administrator.
Qty Uses Decimals	✓		This enables shoppers to order a quantity that is something other than a whole number. For example, 1.5 pounds of coffee.

Field	Appears in Catalog	Manage Products	Product	Inventory	Appears in System	Configuration	Catalog	Inventory	Explanation
Stock Availability	✓		Magento automatically sets this to **In Stock** or **Out of Stock** based upon the quantity in stock, and the minimum quantity for the item's status to be In Stock. However, you can override this by changing the field yourself. For example, suppose you are out of stock and want to sell a floor model. The floor model is not part of your stock. Therefore, you don't want to add it to your quantity in stock. But because your quantity in stock is zero, Magento won't let you take orders for this Product. You could set Stock Availability to Yes, and that would enable you to take an order for the Product.

Time for action: Setting the global and Product inventory options

1. If this is the first Product that you have added, navigate to **System | Configuration | Catalog | Inventory** and set the global default values. If you open the system configuration page in a new tab, you can keep the Product's **Inventory** tab open while you do this.

2. Under the Product's **Inventory** tab, either select the default value for each field or enter a value to override the default.

What just happened?

At this point, you have set global inventory options for your Products. You also have set the inventory options for at least one individual Product. These settings will determine whether a Product is marked as In Stock. At this point you will be reminded to re-order, how much a customer can order, and other related functions.

Part 7: The Categories tab

You can select more than one Category for a Product.

Time for action: Selecting Categories

> ***1.*** Under the **Categories** tab, select the Categories in which this Product will reside as shown in the following screenshot:

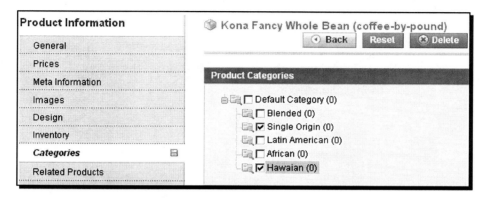

What just happened?

By putting your Product into at least one Category, you made it a part of your online catalog. When a customer explores that Category, the customer will see the Product among those listed in that Category.

Covered elsewhere: Promotions

The remaining tabs are optional. These tabs are used to promote this and related Products. They are covered in Chapter 7.

Summing up

So far, we have:

1. Created Categories.
2. Created Attributes.
3. Created an Attribute Set.
4. Created a Tax Rule.
5. Added a Product.

As you can see from the list, the largest part of adding a Product is the work that comes before you actually add it. It is more efficient to create all the Categories, Attributes, and Tax Rules that you will need before you start adding Products. However, that rarely happens in the real world. When adding a Product, you should be prepared to create Categories, Attributes, and Tax Rules as needed.

Pop quiz

1. Which of the following cannot be changed once you've created a Product?

   a. The Product Name.

   b. The Product Type (simple, compound, and so on).

   c. The Category to which you've assigned the Product.

2. Which two tabs must be filled in, at a minimum, before a Product can be saved?

   a. General

   b. Images

   c. Inventory

   d. Meta Information

   e. Pricing

3. For a Product to be available for purchase, its Status must be set to:

   a. In Stock

   b. Available

   c. Enabled

4. For a Product to show up in your catalog and in search results, you must set its:

   a. Status

   b. Availability

   c. Visibility

Summary

In this chapter, we saw how to add a Product and the Product Information. In the next chapter, we will see what parts of the standard store layout need to be modified, and what parts can be left untouched. Remember that the purpose of this quick-start guide is to get you selling as soon as possible. So, we will not cover extensive customizing of your Magento store. Instead, we will cover only the customizing that is needed.

6
Minimum Customization of Your Store's Appearance

When you install Magento, it creates a default storefront. This storefront uses some of Magento's optional features, such as callouts, to display ads and a newsletter subscription on the front page. It also uses a fictional logo and a welcome message on the front page. All of these features need to be customized for your storefront.

Let's see what our store looks like so far. We will look at both a Category page and the front page.

Our store so far

Let's look at the features of the default Magento store. Later in the chapter, we will learn how to customize each of these.

The default Category page

The default Category page contains many features in common with the default front page, and some that are unique to the Category page.

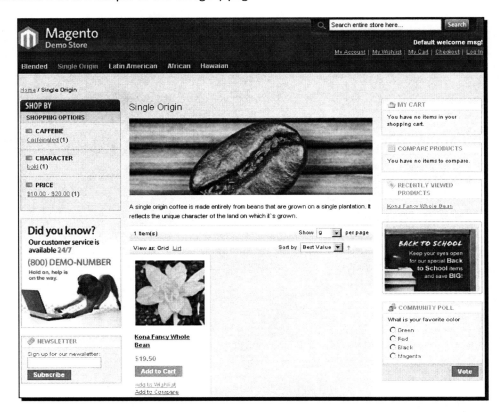

The Layered Navigation Menu

Notice the **Shop By** block in the upper left corner? This is the Layered Navigation Menu. This menu holds the Attributes that we designated as filterable. If this Category had any Child Categories, they would also appear in the Layered Navigation Menu.

Blocks: My Cart, Compare Products, and Recently Viewed Products

These blocks appear by default. The Magento Designer's Guide contains extensive instructions on how to customize the content and layout of your store pages. However, you do not need to customize these blocks for your store to function. Therefore, for this quick-start guide, we will not learn how to customize these standard blocks.

 The Magento Designer's Guide can be found at http://www.magentocommerce.com/design_guide.

Callouts

In the default layout, you can see two callouts on each catalog page: **Did you know?** and **Back to School**. These are the graphics on the left and right. Obviously, these callouts are not appropriate for most stores. We will learn how to remove or replace them with callouts that are appropriate for your store.

Newsletter

Magento's default front page contains a block that enables your customers to sign up for your newsletter. We will learn how to hide this block.

Community Poll

Magento's default front page contains a block that displays a single-question survey, or a poll. We will learn how to hide this block.

Welcome message

In the upper right corner of the page, notice **Default welcome msg!**. We will learn how to customize this welcome message.

Store name

In the upper left corner of the page, notice the store name, **Magento Demo Store**. We will learn how to customize the store name and logo.

The default front page

The default front page is simpler than the default Catalog page. However, it does have some links at the bottom of the page that are also on the catalog pages as shown in the following screenshot:

The default About Us and Customer Service pages

The default **About Us** and **Customer Service** pages contain dummy text and a graphic that you can edit as shown in the following screenshot:

Later, we will learn how to customize these pages. Because the process for customizing the **About Us** and **Customer Service** pages is the same, we cover them together.

The Site Map, Search Terms, Advanced Search, and Contact Us links

Like almost everything else in Magento, you can customize these links. However, you may not need to customize them for your store to function. We will not cover customizing these links in this quick-start guide.

Customize the Layered Navigation Menu

Notice that the Layered Navigation Menu enables the shopper to filter Products by three Attributes: **Caffeine**, **Character**, and **Price**.

In the following screenshot of the **Manage Attributes** page, you can see two of the Attributes that we created: **caffeine** and **character**. They have been designated as **Filterable** as shown in the following screenshot:

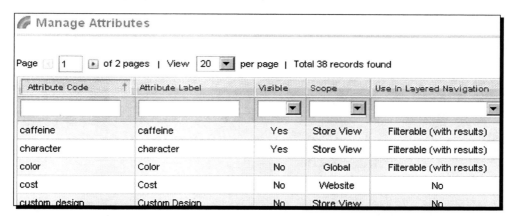

Because these two Attributes are filterable, and not blank, they appear in the Layered Navigation Menu. Remember, only Anchor Categories appear in the Layered Navigation Menu, and then you will see the **filterable** Attributes under those Categories.

You can also see one of Magento's default Attributes, **color**, which is also **filterable**. However, **color** does not appear in the **Shop By** block because we did not make it visible, as you can see from the **No** option in the third column.

Most store owners choose to use the Layered Navigation Menu. If you don't want to use it, you can edit your site's templates to remove that block. However, that is unnecessarily complicated. Instead, simply make all of the Attributes that you use *not filterable*, and the block will disappear.

Customize the Callouts

Let's look at how we can customize the default callouts. Notice that the callouts display in the left and right columns:

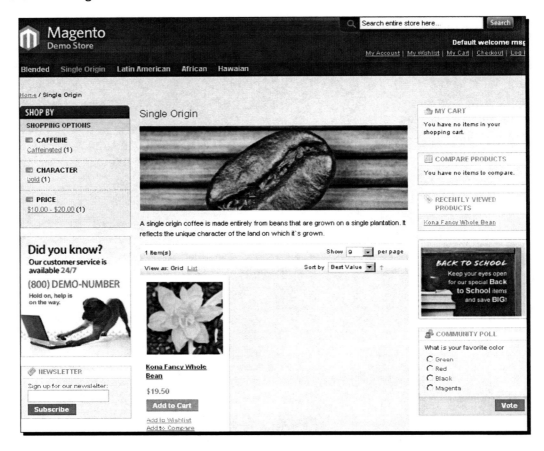

Now look at the default front page. Notice that it does not have a column to the left of the main area. Therefore, the left callout is not displayed on the front page. However, the right column and the right callout are displayed on the front page as shown in the following screenshot:

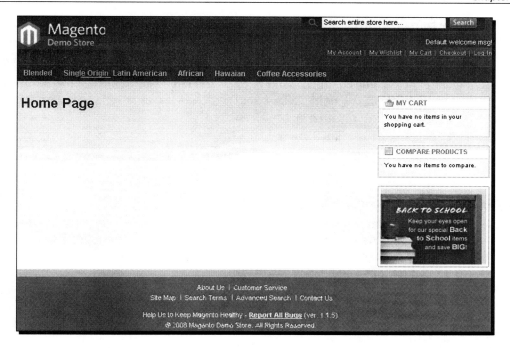

The left callout, which does not appear on the front page, links to your store's Shopping Cart.

To customize these callouts, you will need to do two things:

1. Replace the default graphic for each callout.
2. Replace the default alt text for each callout.

Both are covered in the next section.

Time for action: Replacing the default graphic for a callout

1. Before replacing a graphic for a callout, you should create its replacement. The following default callout graphics is 195-pixels wide:

2. Make sure that you have named the new graphic **col_right_callout.jpg** or **col_left_callout.jpg**, whichever one you are replacing.

3. Navigate to the Magento directory **\skin\frontend\default\default\images\media**.

4. Rename the existing **col_right_callout.jpg** or **col_left_callout.jpg** to something else, such as **ORIGINAL_col_right_callout.jpg**.This preserves the original graphic so that you can roll back to the original condition.

5. Copy your new graphic into **\skin\frontend\default\default\images\media** and name it **col_right_callout.jpg** or **col_left_callout.jpg**, whichever one you are replacing.

Replacing the default alt text for a callout

If your customer's browser is unable to display a graphic, it will display the alternative text for that graphic instead. We call this **alt text**. Also, search engines use a graphic's alt text to help them classify a page. When you replace the graphic for your callout(s), you should also replace the alt text for those graphics.

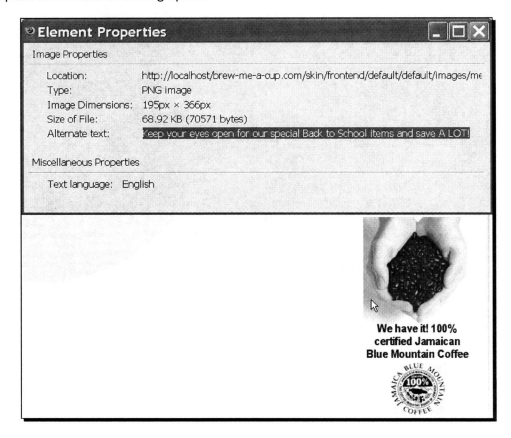

Time for action: Replacing the alt text for the right callout

1. Navigate to the Magento directory **\app\design\frontend\default\default\template\callouts**.

2. Locate the file **right_col.phtml**.

3. Before changing the file, make a duplicate of it. Name it to something like **ORIGINAL_right_col.phtml**.

4. Open the file in a text editor such as WordPad, or in an HTML editor such as DreamWeaver.

5. In the text file, locate the alt text as shown in the following screenshot:

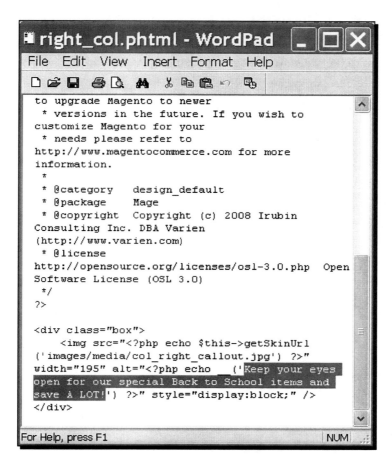

6. Replace the alt text with your own, as shown in the following screenshot:

```
<div class="box">
    <img src="<?php echo $this->getSkinUrl
('images/media/col_right_callout.jpg') ?>"
width="195" alt="<?php echo    ('We have genuine
Blue Mountain Jamaican Coffee certified by the
Jamaican Coffee Board') ?>"
style="display:block;" />
</div>
```

7. Save the file.

Time for action: Replacing the alt text and the link for the left callout

1. Navigate to the Magento directory **\app\design\frontend\default\default\layout**.

2. Locate the file **catalog.xml**.

3. Before changing the file, make a duplicate of it. Name it to something like **ORIGINAL_catalog.xml**.

4. Open the file in a text editor such as WordPad, or in an HTML editor such as DreamWeaver.

5. Locate the default alt text. An easy way to do this is to use the search for **(800) DEMO-NUMBER**.

```
<!--
Default layout, loads most of the pages
-->

    <default>

        <!-- Mage_Catalog -->
        <reference name="top.menu">
            <block type="catalog/navigation" name="catalog.topnav"
template="catalog/navigation/top.phtml"/>
        </reference>
        <reference name="left">
            <block type="core/template"
name="left.permanent.callout" template="callouts/left_col.phtml">
                <action method="setImgSrc"><src>
images/media/col_left_callout.jpg</src></action>
                <action method="setImgAlt" translate="alt"
module="catalog"><alt>Our customer service is available 24/7. Call
us at (800) DEMO-NUMBER.</alt></action>
                <action method="setLinkUrl"><url>checkout/cart</url>
</action>
            </block>
        </reference>
        <reference name="right">
            <block type="core/template" before="cart_sidebar"
name="catalog.compare.sidebar"
template="catalog/product/compare/sidebar.phtml"/>
            <block type="core/template"
name="right.permanent.callout" template="callouts/right_col.phtml"/>
        </reference>
        <reference name="footer_links">
            <action method="addLink" translate="label title"
module="catalog" ifconfig="catalog/seo/site_map"><label>Site Map
</label><url helper="catalog/map/getCategoryUrl" /><title>Site Map
</title></action>
```

6. Replace the alt text with your own.

7. In the next line, notice the link: **checkout/cart**. Replace this with a link of your choice. For example, you could use one of the following links:

To link to this page in your store:	Replace the default link with this text:
Customer Service	customer-service
Contact Us	contacts

8. Save the file.

What just happened?

You just replaced the graphics, alt text, and links for the callouts. To do this, you needed to go outside of Magento and work with files directly in Magento's directory. You might not see a change in your page yet, which we will address in the next section.

Turning off the cache and testing the page

At this point, if you display and refresh a page, you probably won't see the new link. Why would Magento still display the old link for the callout? Let's take a quick detour from customizing the store and talk about Magento's page cache.

As we performed the customizations, we had to navigate through the many folders that make up your Magento installation. There are thousands of files in Magento. When you view a Magento page, you see the result of Magento assembling many different files and displaying them together. Assembling a page takes time and processing power.

Magento holds pages that it displays in a separate storage area called the **cache**. For example, suppose a shopper navigates to the **Single Origin Coffees** category page. Magento will assemble this page, display it for the shopper, and store the page in its cache. When the next shopper asks for the Single Origin Coffees category page, Magento retrieves the page from its cache. This is faster than assembling the page again.

Magento's cache speeds up the display of pages reducing the load on the server. However, it has a disadvantage. After you customize your store, Magento might hold on to the old versions of pages. Instead of assembling the latest version of a page, sometimes Magento will display the old, cached version. To correct this, we usually turn off the cache while customizing our storefront. When we finish with our changes, we turn the cache on again.

Time for action: Turning the page cache off

1. From the Admin interface, select **System | Cache Management**.

2. You can select which types of information Magento will cache. However, when performing the basic customization on your site, it is usually easiest to enable and disable all of them at once.

3. From the drop-down menu next to **All Cache**, select **Disable** or **Enable**.

4. Click on the **Save cache settings** button.

5. Refresh the page that you are testing.

What just happened?

By turning off Magento's cache, you have ensured that any changes you make to your pages will show up as soon as you refresh them in your browser. However, you have also increased the load on your web server. When you're done with developing your site, you will want to turn the cache back on.

Disabling the Newsletter or Poll

Customizing and using the newsletter feature is covered later book when we discuss about customer relationships . If you are not going to publish a newsletter soon, you might want to disable this feature for now. Also, if you are not going to customize the poll, you should disable it.

Time for action: Disabling the Newsletter or Poll

1. Go to **System | Configuration | Advanced | Advanced**. You should see the **Disable modules output** page.

2. Locate the module labeled **Mage_Newsletter** and/or **Mage_Poll**, and select **Disable**.

3. Click on the **Save Config** button.

What just happened?

When you refresh your front page, the newsletter and/or poll block should disappear. Later, you can customize and re-enable them.

Customize the welcome message

From the Admin interface, select **System | Configuration | General | Design**.

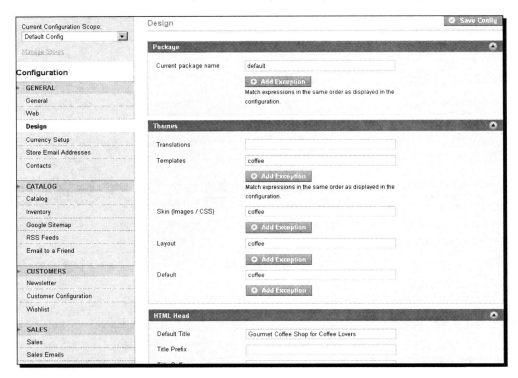

This page enables you to customize several items. For now, let's look at the ones that are necessary.

The HTML Head section

Recall that we talked about metadata when creating a product. Metadata helps search engines to determine the content of a web page, and to categorize the page. The **HTML Head** section enables you to customize the metadata for your entire store. The data you enter into the fields on this page will appear in the header of each page in your store. Your shoppers won't see this data, but search engines will.

Default Title

If a page in your site does not have a customized title, then it will use the title given here. For example, when you created products, each Product page used the name of the Product as its title. All of Magento's built-in pages have their own titles, and so this field should not affect your system unless you create custom pages.

Default Description

This is your store's description. Some search sites will display this to their searchers. Treat this like a one-sentence marketing piece designed to entice searchers to click through to your store.

Default Keywords

Enter keywords that will help search engines to classify your site.

The Header section

The fields in this section are used to customize the logo and the welcome message.

Logo Image Src and Alt Text

By default, Magento looks in `\skin\frontend\default\default\images\logo.gif` for the store's logo. The graphic is 157-by-47 pixels in size. The easiest way to customize your store's logo is to make a direction replacement, the same size and file name, and replace the existing one.

The field **Logo Image Alt** holds the alt text for the logo. This will be displayed if the graphic is not displayed.

Welcome Text

Enter your customized welcome message into this field.

The Footer section

On this page, you can change the **Copyright** notice. This is the last line in the previous screenshot.

The links **About Us**, **Customer Service**, and **Contact Us** are customized elsewhere, as is the message immediately above the copyright notice.

There is also a field on the configuration page for **Miscellaneous HTML**. This enables you to add any HTML code immediately below the copyright. For example, you can add Google Analytics, or some other code, to help you track visitors on your site.

Using new themes

Your store's layout, terminology, colour scheme, typestyles, and images are controlled by its theme. Creating an entirely new theme for your site is beyond the scope of this book. Covering it will require an entire book by itself. However, you can easily replace your site's default theme with a theme that someone has built for you. In addition to many paid themes, you can find plenty of free themes on the web as well.

The files for your store's theme reside in these two directories:

1. `/app/design/frontend/default/default/`—This directory contains the layout, translations for the labels and terms, and templates.

2. `/skin/frontend/default/default/`—This directory contains images, style sheets, and JavaScript for the blocks.

The last part of those paths, `/default`, is the name of the theme that comes with Magento, default theme. When you install a new theme, you will place its files under `/app/design/frontend/default` and `/skin/frontend/default`. For example, I downloaded the free Linen theme from `www.magthemes.com`, and copied its files into `/app/design/frontend/default/linen` and `/skin/frontend/default/linen`.

When I unzipped the package for the Linen theme, it contained these directories:

- `/skin/frontend/LinenTheme/default`
- `/app/design/frontend/LinenTheme/default`

Time for action: Installing a theme

To install this theme, perform the following steps:

1. Rename `skin/frontend/LinenTheme/default` to `skin/frontend/LinenTheme/linen`.

2. Rename `app/design/frontend/LinenTheme/default` to `app/design/frontend/LinenTheme/linen`.

3. Copy the directory `linen` and its subdirectories from `/skin/frontend/LinenTheme/linen` into the Magento directory, `/skin/frontend/default/`. Your directories now look like the following.

4. Copy the directory `linen` and its subdirectories from `/app/design/frontend/` `LinenTheme/linen` into the Magento directory, `/app/design/frontend/` `default/linen`. Your directories now look like the following:

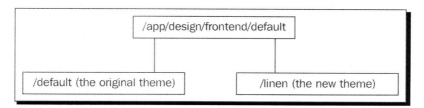

5. In the Admin interface, navigate to **System | Configuration | General | Design**. You should see a section on that page labeled as **Themes**:

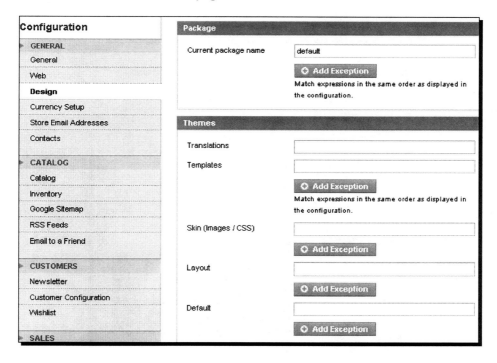

6. In the fields **Templates**, **Skin**, **Layout**, and **Default**, type the name of the directory for the new theme. In this case, type **linen** into each of those fields:

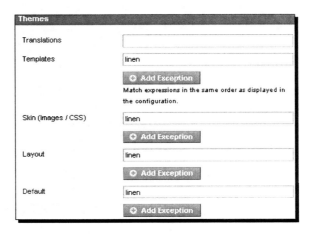

7. Save the configuration.

8. Refresh the frontend. You should see the new theme applied to your store as shown in the following screenshot:

What just happened?

Notice that this theme changed the store's appearance in several ways. Now, only one callout is displayed, and it is not one of the callouts that we customized. Also, the logo has changed. It is no longer the one which we customized. If we want to preserve the graphics that we customized, we need to move them into the /images directory of the new theme.

Changing your store's name

Out of the box, Magento gives your store the name **Default Store View**. This name appears in several places, such as when a customer creates an account on your site.

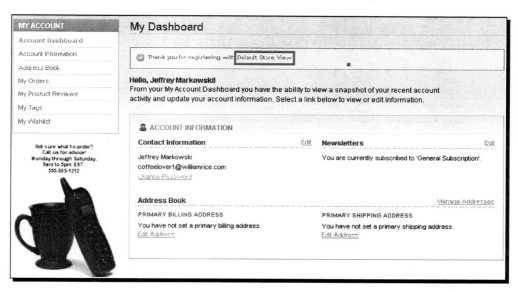

You should change this to your store's name.

Time for action: Change your store's name

1. From the Admin interface, select **System | Manage Stores**.
2. Click the link for **Default Store View**. The **Store View Information** page is displayed as shown in the following screenshot:

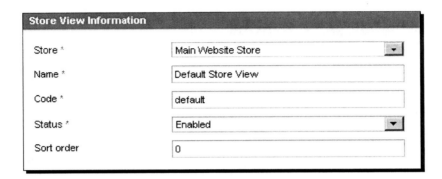

3. In the **Name** field, enter the name for your store that you want customers to see.

4. Click on **Save Store View**.

What just happened?

Now whenever Magento displays your store name, it will show the text that you entered in the **Name** field.

Summary

Magento enables you to customize almost every aspect of your store's appearance. A complete customization requires you to create a new theme, which is beyond the scope of this book. However, you can easily customize the default Magento installation in significant ways. Without getting into making a new theme, you can still make your store unique.

If you plan on customizing the logo, callouts, or any other graphics; and installing a new theme (either free or paid for), install the new theme first. Once the installation is complete, customize the elements of the new theme. If you customize the elements on your store's default theme, and then replace the default theme with a new theme, you will have wasted time customizing the default theme.

7
Beyond Simple Products

In Chapter 5 you learned how to add Simple Products to your store. Magento enables you to go beyond that and offer more complex Products. These include Related Products, Grouped Products, and Configurable Products

When you offer Related Products with a Simple Product, they are displayed in the Related Products block when a customer views the Simple Product. Related Products are meant to be bought along with a Simple Product. Consider using this feature when you want to sell accessories or add-ons for a Simple Product.

Grouped Products are groups of Products that are meant to be purchased together such as a suit jacket and suit pants.

A **Configurable Product** is a Product in which the customer gets to choose an attribute(s) of the Product such as the color, size, or material.

You can also offer discounts for buying in quantity, by using tiered pricing.

Related Products

You can display Related Products for any Product in your catalog. These will appear in the Related Products block. Related Products are meant to be purchased in addition to the Product the customer is viewing.

In our demonstration store, we sell several kinds of whole-bean coffee. For each of these Products, we want to display a coffee grinder as the Related Product:

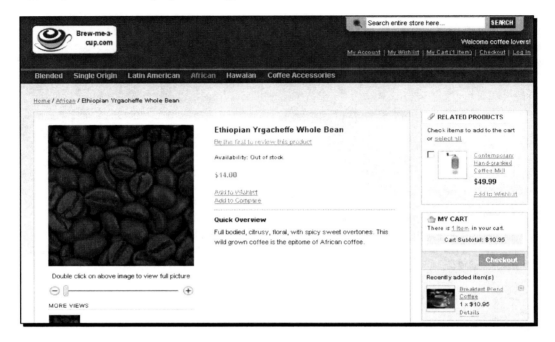

By default, the **RELATED PRODUCTS** block appears in the upper right corner of the page. On web pages, this is considered a highly visible spot. The block appears only if you have designated at least one related Product.

This block will not appear if the customer is viewing a Configurable Product, even if one of its configurations has a Related Product. The block appears only for Simple Products.

Notice the checkbox next to the Related Product. If a customer selects a Related Product and adds the main Product to the Shopping Cart, the Related Product will also be added. If (s)he doesn't add the main Product, the Related Product will not be added.

Time for action: Adding related Product(s) to a Product

Follow these steps to add related Products to a Product.

1. From the Admin interface, select **Catalog | Manage Products**.

2. The list of Products in your store will be displayed.

3. Click anywhere on the Product that you want to edit. Or, you can click the **Edit** link for that Product:

4. When the Product's page is displayed, select the **Related Products** tab. to display a search box. You will use this to search for, and select, the Related Products.

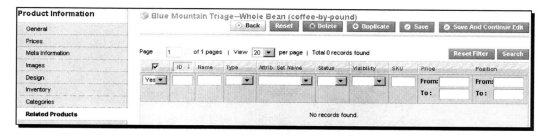

5. To display all of the Products in your store, click on **Reset Filter**. To search for a specific product, enter the criteria and click on **Search**.

6. To select a Related Product, click the appropriate box to place a check mark in the first column as shown in the following screenshot.

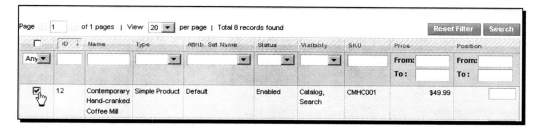

7. If this Product has several Related Products, specify the order in which they will appear by entering a number in the **Position** field, which is in the column to the far right.

8. Click on **Save**.

What just happened?

The Related Products that you specified will now be displayed whenever a customer views this Product.

Grouped Products

A Grouped Product is a shortcut for simultaneously adding several Products to the Shopping Cart. A Grouped Product is not really a Product. It is a group of Products that is displayed together. A Grouped Product can include both Simple and Configurable Products.

In the following example, you can see that our **Single Origin Sampler** consists of three separate Simple Products:

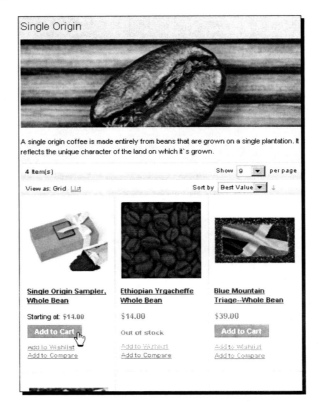

When a customer clicks on the Grouped Product's name, or the **Add to Cart** button, (s)he is taken to the Grouped Product's page:

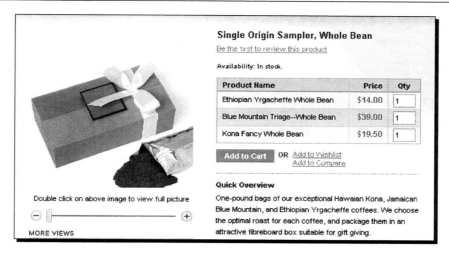

On this page, the customer chooses the quantity and adds the Grouped Product to the Shopping Cart. Notice that a Grouped Product's page clearly lists the individual Products that make up the Grouped Product. Also, notice that the system has filled in a quantity for the customer. When you create a Grouped Product, you specify a default quantity for each of its Products. While the quantity is initially set, the customer can override it and enter new quantities.

Creating a Grouped Product

The process for creating a Grouped Product is almost the same as for a Simple Product. It differs the most only in the last part of the process, when you select the Simple Products that will belong to this Group.

Time for action: Creating a Blank Grouped Product

1. Make sure that you have created all of the individual Products that will be a part of the Grouped Product.

2. From the Admin interface, select **Catalog | Manage Products**.

3. Click on **Add Product**. The **Create Product Settings** page is displayed as shown in the following screenshot:

4. Select an **Attribute Set**. You do not need to select the same Attribute Set as the individual Products that make up the Grouped Product. You can choose any Attribute Set.

5. For **Product Type**, select **Grouped Product**.

6. Click on **Continue**. The **Product Information** page is displayed as shown in the following screenshot:

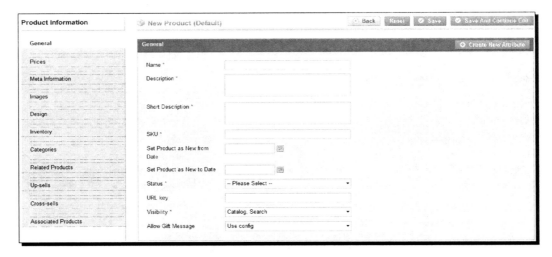

Notice that there are no tabs for Weight and Price. As the Grouped Product is a collection of individual Products, its weight and price are the sum of the individual Products.

The procedure for creating a Group Product is almost identical to creating a Simple Product. Because you need to create several individual Products before creating a Group Product, these instructions assume that you know how to create a Product. Therefore, they will focus on what is unique about creating a Grouped Product. If you don't understand any part of these instructions, consider reviewing the procedure for creating a Simple Product explained in Chapter 5.

What just happened?

You now have a blank Grouped Product ready, in which you can fill in the details. After you complete the tabs for this Grouped Product, you will add Simple Products to this group. The **General** tab is selected for you. Let's begin there.

Time for action: Completing the General tab

When Magento displays a product in your store, that product appears on its own page. Most of the information that your shoppers see on that page is entered here, on the **General** tab.

Notice that several fields on this page are marked with red asterisks. These fields are required, so you must fill them.

 You must fill in the required fields under the **General** tab before leaving the New Product page. Even if you save your work, the product will not be added to your store if you haven't filled in the required fields.

1. Enter **Name, Description,** and **Short Description**.

    The way these fields function is similar to the fields for Simple Product. Your customers will see the product **Name** at the top of the product's page. The **Short Description** field appears below that, in the section labeled **Quick Overview**. The **Description** field appears below that.

2. Enter a unique **SKU**.

    A Grouped Product has an SKU, just like a Simple Product. However, when a customer adds a Grouped Product to the Shopping Cart, the individual Product's SKUs are added to the cart. The Grouped Product's SKU is not added to the Cart.

2. Optionally, enter dates for **Set Product as New from/to Date**.

A new product can be included in the new product display, RSS feed, and/or an email announcement. Setting dates in the fields for **Set product as new from/to date** makes the product new to Magento. If you use any of these features, you will need to fill in the date fields. However, if you don't highlight the new products in your store, you can safely leave these fields blank.

If any of the individual Products that make up the Grouped Product are new, they will also appear as new in addition to the Grouped Product.

3. Select a **Status** for this Group.

Enabled makes this product active and displays it in your store. **Disabled** makes this product inactive and hides it from shoppers. It is good practice to keep a product **Disabled** until you've filled out all the tabs and double-checked your work.

4. Enter a **URL key**.

This field functions in the same it does for a Simple Product. The **URL key** field creates a search engine friendly URL. Because a URL cannot have spaces or special characters, you cannot use it in this field. If you leave this field blank, Magento will generate a search engine friendly URL for you based on the product's **Name**.

5. Select the **Visibility** for this Group.

This field determines if the product will not display at all in your site (**Nowhere**), display on the pages of your site (**Catalog**), show up in search results (**Search**), or both (**Catalog, Search**). Note that although a product's **Status** is set to **Enabled**, your shoppers won't be able to see or find that product if you have its **Visibility** set to **Nowhere**.

6. Select the setting for **Allow Gift Message**.

This field determines whether customers can add a gift message to this product during checkout. **Yes** and **No** are self-explanatory. **Use config** means that for this product, Magento will use the sitewide setting for gift messages. You will find that setting under **System | Sales | Sales | Gift Messages**.

7. Save and Continue

In the upper right corner of the **New Product** page, there are two Save buttons:

Save will save what you have entered in this tab, and advance you to the next tab. **Save and Continue Edit** will save the information that you entered, but keep you on the same tab.

What just happened?

You have completed one of the required tabs for a Grouped Product. The only thing that is required to create the product is to select the Simple Products that will be part of the Grouped Product.

Time for action: Completing the Meta Information tab

Use **Meta Keywords** and **Meta Description** as opportunities to optimize the page for search engines.

1. For **Meta Title**, enter the title for this Product page. The title should include search terms that customers will use when searching for this kind of a product.

2. For **Meta Keywords**, enter keywords that describe this Product. The keywords should be the search terms that customers are likely to use when searching for this kind of product.

3. For **Meta Description**, enter a single sentence or phrase that describes the Product. If a potential customer finds this Product through a search engine, such as Google or ask.com, what description would you like the customer to see? That is what you should enter here.

What just happened?

The meta information that you entered for this product will not make any visible difference on the product's page. However, the meta information will be used by search engines to categorize the product's page more accurately.

Time for action: Uploading images

1. On the **Product Information** page, select the **Images** tab.

2. Click on **Browse Files...**. In the dialog box that appears, select one file to upload.

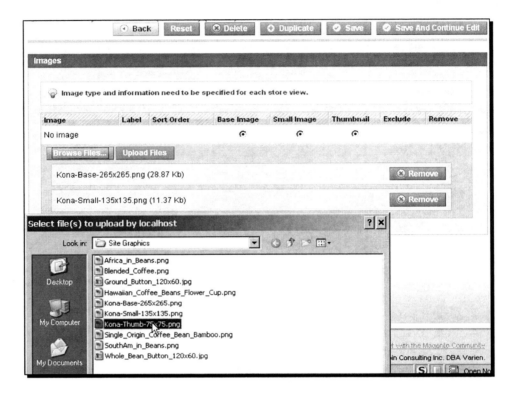

3. After selecting the image, click on the **Open** or **OK** button in the dialog box.

4. If you want the same image to be used for base, small, and thumbnail, you can move to the next step. If you want to use separate images for each of the three images, then click on **Browse Files...** and select the appropriate images.

5. After you select all the images that you want for this Product, click on **Upload Files.** The files will be uploaded to the **Images** page.

   In our example, only one image has been uploaded for the product. It will be used for all three image sizes. For coffee, it did not make sense to have multiple images because there is not much to show about this product.

6. Select the image you want for the **Base Image**, **Small Image**, and **Thumbnail Image** by clicking the radio buttons shown in the following screenshot:

7. To exclude an image type, click on the radio button in the top row for **No Image**. This means that wherever Magento would have used that image size, no image will be displayed. For example, the thumbnail image appears in the Shopping Cart. If you select **No Image** for the **Thumbnail Image**, then no image will be added when this is placed in the Shopping Cart. You might use **No Image** when you are selling something for which an image doesn't make sense. For example, if you're selling a repair service you might not need an image.

8. Enter a **Label** for each image. This will be used as the "alt text" for that image.

9. Click on **Save And Continue Edit**.

What just happened?

The image(s) that you uploaded will be displayed on the Grouped Product's page. The **Design** tab is next on the menu. We will skip that tab because it is beyond the scope of a beginner's guide. Instead, proceed to the **Inventory** tab.

Time for action: Completing the Inventory tab

For a Grouped Product, there are only two settings under the **Inventory** tab: **Manage Stock** and **Stock Availability** as shown in the following screenshot:

All of the other settings that you normally find under this tab are managed under individual Products.

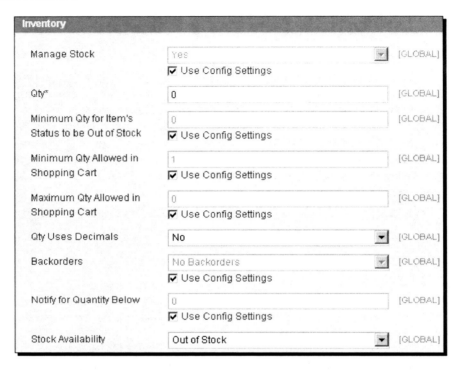

1. If you want to track the inventory for this Grouped Product, set **Manage Stock** to **Yes**.

2. To make the Grouped Product available to shoppers select **In Stock** for **Stock Availability**. This makes the Grouped Product available. The individual Simple Products must also be in stock. If any of the Simple Products are unavailable, the shopper can still add the remaining ones to the Shopping Cart by adding the Grouped Product.

What just happened?

In this part, you made the Grouped Product available to shoppers. The actual inventory numbers will be managed under individual Simple Products.

Time for action: Assigning a Category

1. Under the **Categories** tab, select the Categories in which this Grouped Product will reside. This does not need to be the same category as the individual Products in the Group.

What just happened?

In this step, you made the Grouped Product available under a specific category. The individual Simple Products might still be available under different Categories if you choose to sell them separately.

Time for action: Selecting Associated Products

Under the **Associated Products** tab you select the Products that are part of this Group.

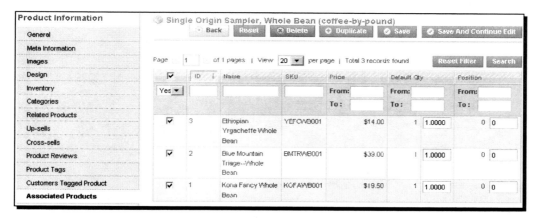

The previous screenshot shows what this tab looks like after you have added **Associated Products**. When you first select this tab, there will be no **Associated Products**.

1. Click on **Reset Filter** to view all products, or to find specific products, enter your search criterion and click on **Search**. This causes the Products in your store to be displayed in the list.

2. To select a Product, click to place a check mark in the first column.

3. Enter a default quantity for the Product. This will pre-fill the quantity field, **Qty**, when the customer selects this Group.

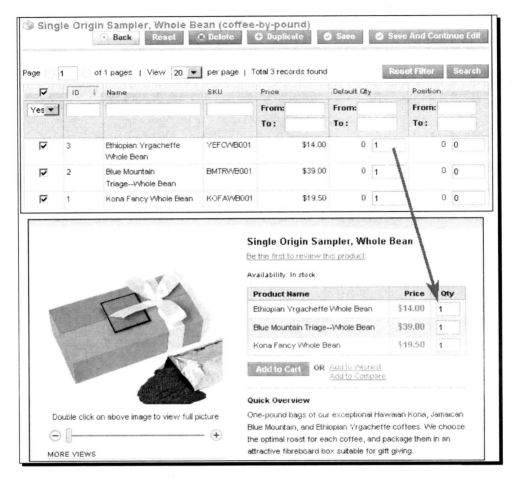

4. Use the **Position** field to determine the order in which the Products should be displayed.

5. Click on **Save**.

What just happened?

You just completed the last step in creating a Grouped Product. Now when a shopper visits the page for the product, (s)he will see a picture and description for the Group. (S)he will also see the individual Simple Products that will be added to the cart if the Group Product is added.

Configurable Products

A Configurable Product is one where the customer gets to choose an attribute of the Product. For example, a pair of shoes is a Configurable Product if the customer gets to choose the size. Likewise, a shirt is also a Configurable Product if the customer can choose the size and colour. In our demo store, we will create a Configurable Product by enabling customers to choose the **grind** for a coffee.

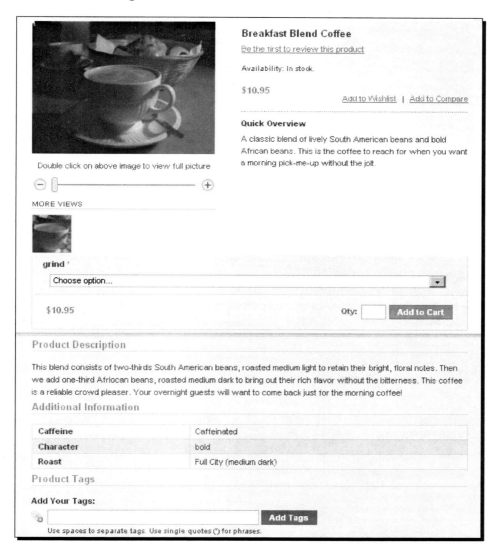

A Configurable Product is actually a collection of Simple Products. Think about a shoe example. In the inventory, the store has many different sizes of the same model of shoe. Each size is in a different shoebox, and has a different SKU. Each size is, essentially, a different Product. When a shopper selects a specific size, (s)he is really selecting a specific Product with its own, unique SKU.

This means that for every choice you give your customers for a Configurable Product, you need to create a Simple Product. For example, suppose you sell a shirt in the following configurations:

Size	Color	SKU
small	blue	shsmbl
medium	blue	shmebl
small	red	shsmre
medium	red	shmere
large	red	shlare

In this case, you would allow the customer to choose two Attributes for this Configurable Product: size and color. Hence, you would create five Simple Products.

Creating a Configurable Product

Before creating a Configurable Product, you should plan the Simple Products that you want to be included in the Configurable Product.

Time for action: Designating some Attributes as configurable

This section assumes that you know how to create and use Attributes. This was covered in Chapter 3.

1. From the Admin interface, select **Catalog | Attributes | Manage Attributes**. A list of all Attributes in the system is displayed.

2. Click on the Attribute that you want to make configurable. The **Attribute Properties** page is displayed as shown in the next screenshot:

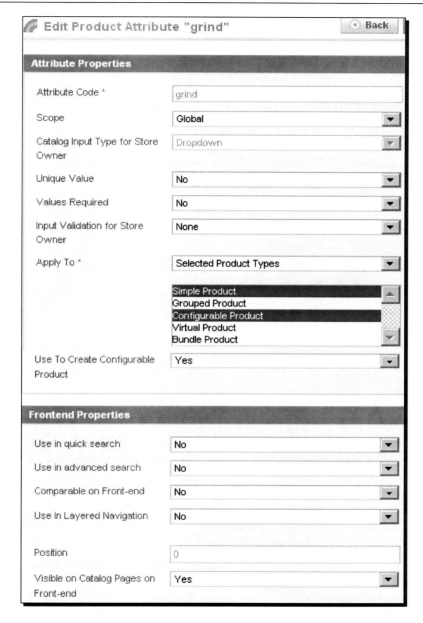

3. To make this Attribute configurable, set the **Scope** to **Global**. The Attribute needs to be available everywhere in your site.

4. Set the **Input Type** to **Dropdown**. This creates a drop-down list for the customer.

5. Set **Use To Create Configurable Product** to **Yes**.

6. Click on the **Save** button.

7. Make sure that the Attribute Set that you will use for this Configurable Product contains the configurable Attribute(s) that you just set up.

What just happened?

You just designated an Attribute(s) as configurable. Now, you can create a Configurable Product based on that Attribute. This means that your shoppers will be able to choose a value for that Attribute, and they will be shown a Product with that value.

 This next section assumes that you know how to create Products. This was covered in Chapter 5.

You must create the Products that will be associated with this Configurable Product. You will create the first Product in the same way as you would any other Simple Product. If you need complete instructions, refer to the instructions for creating a Simple Product in Chapter 5. The following section contains just the key points that you must remember when creating a Simple Product, which will be a part of a Configurable Product.

After creating the first Simple Product, you will duplicate it and use the duplicate as the starting point for the next Simple Product. This section covers creating the first Simple Product. The next section covers duplicating it and creating the rest of the Simple Products.

Time for action: Creating the first Simple Product that will be associated to the Configurable Product

1. Immediately after clicking the **Create Product** button, the system displays a dialog box where you select the **Attribute Set** and the **Product Type**.

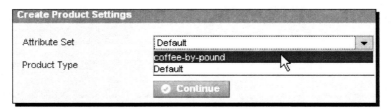

2. You must select an Attribute Set that has one or more configurable Attributes, such as the one that was set up in the previous section.

In our demo store, we selected **coffee-by-pound** because it contains the configurable Attribute, **grind**.

> The Simple Products can differ in more than just the configurable attribute. For example, suppose you sell t-shirts. Maybe all the small shirts are available only in black, and all the medium-sized shirts are available in black and red. In that case, you would make both size and color as configurable attributes. When a customer selects the small size, (s)he would see only black in the color selection column. When (s)he selects the medium size, (s)he would see black and red in the color selection. Both Attributes must be configurable, even if you're using them both on only some of the Simple Products in this Configurable Product.

3. For **Product Type**, select **Simple Product**. Remember, you are creating one of the Products that will be associated with the Configurable Product. You are creating the Configurable Product itself.

4. After you click on the **Continue** button, the Product Information page is displayed. Fill out this page as you would for any Product.

Pay special attention to the setting for the Configurable Atribute(s) that you set. In our demo store, we selected a value for **grind**.

When we create the other Simple Products for this Configurable Product, we will choose a different **grind** for each of them.

5. Make sure that every Product in your store needs a unique **SKU**.

6. Set the **Status** of this Product to **Enabled**, or else it won't be available to your customers.

7. Unlike a normal Simple Product, set the **Visibility** to **Nowhere**. This prevents the Product from having its own listing in your store. If you forget to do this, the Product will show up as both a normal product with its own listing, and as a selection under a Configurable Product. The following screenshot demonstrates that mistake. Notice that all three Simple Products, which will be choices for the Configurable Product, appear by themselves.

When I set the **Visibility** to **Nowhere**, these Products will disappear from the page.

8. Fill in the rest of the information for this Product, just as you would for any other Simple Product. If you need complete instructions, refer to the instructions for creating a Simple Product enlisted in Chapter 5.

9. Save the Product.

What just happened?

You just created the first Simple Product that will be a part of the group of Products that comprise this Configurable Product. Now you are ready to create duplicates of this Product, and use each Duplicate as the starting point for a new Product.

To begin the next part of the procedure, you should keep open the Product that you want to duplicate.

Time for action: Duplicating the first Simple Product and creating other Products

1. Click on **Duplicate**. When the Product is duplicated, you will see a message at the top of the page.

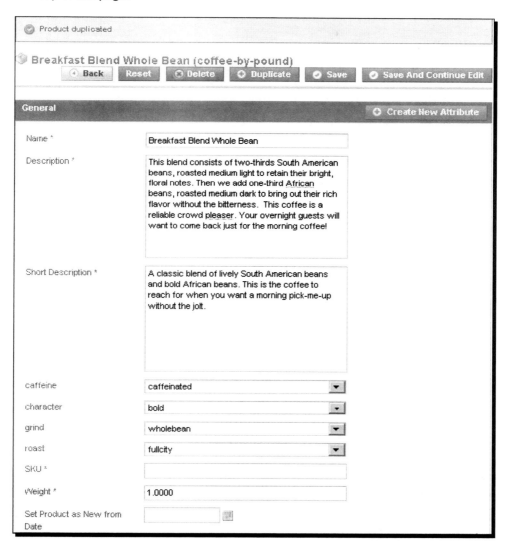

You know that you are working with a duplicate Product, and not the original, because the SKU is blank.

2. For the configurable Attribute, choose a new value.

In our demo store, we chose a new value for **grind**:

3. Enter a unique **SKU** for this Product.

4. Set the **Status** to **Enabled**.

5. If needed, edit the **Name** and **Description**.

6. Under **Inventory**, the **Qty** for the new Product is automatically set to zero, and the **Stock Availability** is set to **Out of Stock**. You must change these.

7. Look through the tabs for any other information that needs to be changed for this new Product. For example, if you changed the **Name** and **Description**, would you also need to change the **Meta Information**? Does this Product look different enough from the others that you will need to upload new **Images** for the product?

8. Save this Product.

9. Repeat as needed, until you have created all of the Products that you need for this Configurable Product.

What just happened?

You have just created Simple Products which will comprise this Configurable Product. When a shopper selects a value for the Configurable Product's attribute, (s)he is essentially selecting one of the Simple Products that you just created.

Time for action: Creating a blank Configurable Product

1. Make sure that you have created all of the individual Products that will be a part of the Configurable Product.

2. From the Admin interface, select **Catalog | Manage Products**.

3. Click on **Add Product**. The **Create Product Settings** page gets displayed.

4. Select an **Attribute Set**. You must select an **Attribute Set** that has one or more configurable Attributes, such as the one that was set up in the previous section.

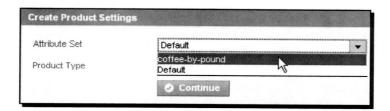

5. For **Product Type**, select **Configurable Product**.

6. Click on **Continue**. You will see a dialog box asking you to select the Configurable Attributes for this Product.

If there are no Configurable Attributes listed, it means the Attribute Set that you selected for this Product contains no Configurable Attributes. Either go back to **Catalog | Attributes | Manage Attributes** and make at least one Attribute configurable, or start over and select an Attribute Set that has a Configurable Attribute.

7. Select the Attribute(s) that you want to be configurable. This will create a drop-down list for that Attribute, enabling the customer to choose a value for the Product.

8. Click on **Continue**. The **Product Information** page is displayed as shown:

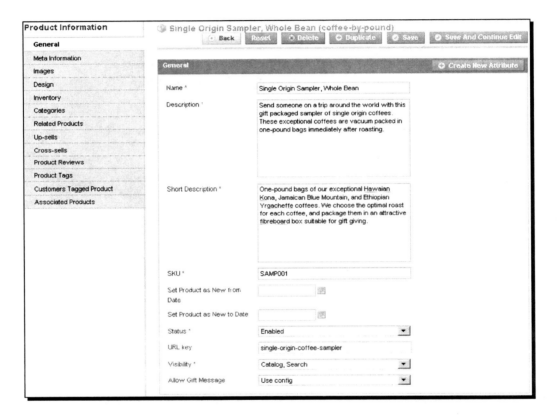

Notice that there is no tab for weight. As the Grouped Product is a collection of individual Products, its weight is the sum of individual Products. The weight will be calculated after the group is added to the Shopping Cart.

The **Prices** tab has only one field, **Not available for purchase with Google Checkout** with **Yes** or **No** as options. Again, the price of the group depends upon the prices of the individual items, and is calculated when the group is added to the Shopping Cart.

The procedure for creating a Configurable Product is almost identical to creating a Simple Product. As you need to create several individual Products before creating a Configurable Product, these instructions assume that you know how to create a Product. Therefore, they will focus on what is unique about creating a Configurable Product. If you don't understand any part of these instructions, consider reviewing the procedure for creating a Simple Product given in Chapter 5.

The **General** tab is selected for you. Let's begin there.

9. Fill in the fields under the **General** tab as you would for any other Product.

10. Enter a unique **SKU**.

11. Set the **Status** to **Enabled**.

12. Unlike the individual Products that make up this Configurable Product, you should set the **Visibility** to **Catalog**, or **Search**, or **Catalog, Search**.

13. Under **Inventory**, the only settings you will see are **Manage Stock** and **Stock Availability**. Set the **Stock Availability** to **In Stock**.

14. Select the **Prices** tab.

15. In the **Price** field, enter the base price for this Product. Later on, you will enter a price modifier for each Associate Product.

For example, suppose you sell shirts in sizes that range from extra-small to extra-extra-large. Further suppose that the price for the extra-small size is $9, small through extra-large is $10, and extra-extra-large is $11. In this field, you would enter a price of $10. Later on, you would enter a price modifier for extra-small of -$1 (negative one dollar) and a price modifier for extra-extra-large of +$1 (positive one dollar).

16. Look through the tabs for any other information that needs to be changed. For example, will you need a different **Name** and **Description** for the Configurable Product? Will you also need to change the **Meta Information**? Do you want to upload an **Image** that shows several versions of the Product?

17. Click on **Save And Continue Edit**.

What just happened?

You just created a Configurable Product, and selected all of the settings needed for that product. You are now ready to select the Simple Products that will comprise this Configurable Product.

Time for action: Associating the Simple Products to the Configurable Product

1. Select the **Associated Products** tab.

At the top of this page you will see sections labeled **Create Simple Associated Product** and **Quick simple product creation**. If you had not created the Simple Products for this Configurable Product, you could use either of these to create a new Product. As you have already created all the needed Products, you can skip these sections. When you need to create a new Simple Product for this Configurable Product, you will have three options:

- ❑ **Duplicate** a Product, as you did earlier.
- ❑ Use **Create Simple Associated Product**.
- ❑ Use **Quick simple product creation**.

The last two options are shortcuts. They are not difficult to learn, however you already know how to use the first option, and it doesn't take much longer than the other two.

At the bottom of the page, you will list all of the Simple Products that use the same Attribute Set as this Configurable Product.

2. Click on **Reset Filter** to show all products or to search for specific products, enter a search criterion and click on **Search**.

This causes the Products that use the same Attribute Set to be displayed in the list. The Products that cannot be associated will be shaded, while the ones that that can will not be shaded.

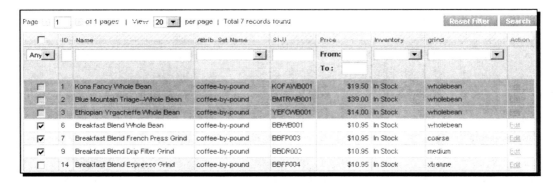

	ID	Name	Attrib. Set Name	SKU	Price	Inventory	grind	Action
Any ▼					From:	▼	▼	
					To :			
☐	1	Kona Fancy Whole Bean	coffee-by-pound	KOFAWB001	$19.50	In Stock	wholebean	
☐	2	Blue Mountain Triage--Whole Bean	coffee-by-pound	BMTRWB001	$39.00	In Stock	wholebean	
☐	3	Ethiopian Yrgacheffe Whole Bean	coffee-by-pound	YEFCWB001	$14.00	In Stock	wholebean	
☑	6	Breakfast Blend Whole Bean	coffee-by-pound	BBWB001	$10.95	In Stock	wholebean	Edit
☑	7	Breakfast Blend French Press Grind	coffee-by-pound	BBFP003	$10.95	In Stock	coarse	Edit
☑	9	Breakfast Blend Drip Filter Grind	coffee-by-pound	BBDR002	$10.95	In Stock	medium	Edit
☐	14	Breakfast Blend Espresso Grind	coffee-by-pound	BBFP004	$10.95	In Stock	xfraine	Edit

Page 1 of 1 pages | View 20 ▼ per page | Total 7 records found — Reset Filter | Search

Looking at the previous screenshot, you can see that **Breakfast Blend Whole Bean** has a **grind** of **wholebean**. The first three Products in the list cannot be associated because they also have a **grind** of **wholebean**. Each Associated Product must have a unique setting for the configurable attributes. That is because when the customer selects a setting for the configurable attribute, the customer should see only one Product. In our example, you can assign only one Associated Product for each of these settings: **wholebean**, **coarse**, **medium**, and **xtrafine**.

3. To select a Product, click to place a check mark in the first column.

4. Click on **Save And Continue Edit**. After saving, Magento takes you to the **General** tab. Return to the **Associated Products** tab.

5. In the **Super product attributes configuration** section, you will see each Configurable Attribute listed.

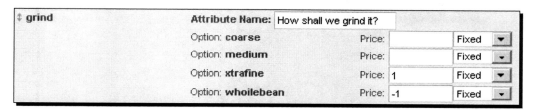

6. In the **Attribute Name** field, enter the text that you want the customer to see when they choose the setting for this Attribute.

7. In the **Price** field for each setting, enter a price modifier.

In our demo store, the result looks like this:

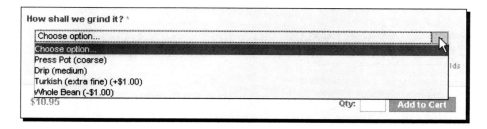

Notice the base price, **$10.95**, in the lower left corner. We entered this under the **Prices** tab. The label, **How shall we grind it?**, was entered under the Attribute Name. You can see the price modifiers for the **Turkish** and **Whole Bean** grinds, which we also entered earlier.

8. Finally, save the Product.

What just happened?

Your Configurable Produce is complete. When customers view this product, they will be able to select different values for the Attribute that you made configurable. When they select one of these values, they will be selecting the individual Simple Product that has a value for that specific Attribute.

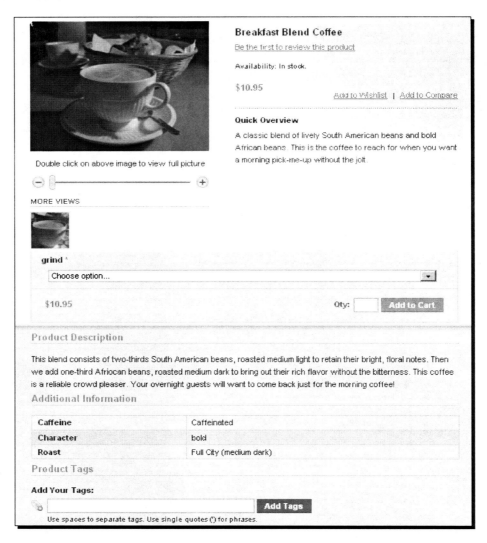

Tiered pricing

Tiered pricing enables you to give special prices for a specified group, or customers, and a specified quantity. It is set under the **Prices** tab.

A tiered price has the following three components:

1. The **Customer Group**: Who gets the special price?
2. The minimum quantity (**Qty**): How much must the customer buy to get the special price?
3. The special **Price**: It is also called the Tier Price.

Giving discounts for minimum quantities to all customers

In the simplest case, you will give a discount to anyone who buys a minimum quantity. In that case, you would create a single tier, and apply the **Tier Price** to **ALL GROUPS**. For example, in the following screenshot of the **Prices** tab, you can see that this tier creates a 15% discount for buying three bags or more:

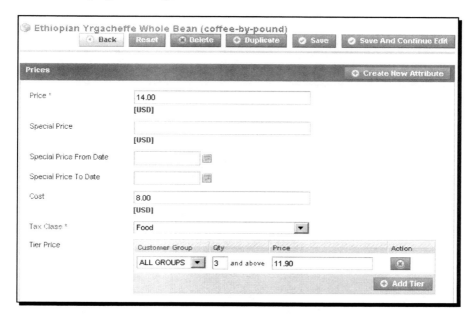

Notice that the normal price is **$14.00** per pound. For the tier price, we wanted to give a 15% discount. So, we calculated that $14.00 minus 15% is **$11.90** per pound. Also, notice that the **Customer Group** is set to **ALL GROUPS**.

In a more complex case, you could use multiple tiers. Once again, these tiers apply to all customers.

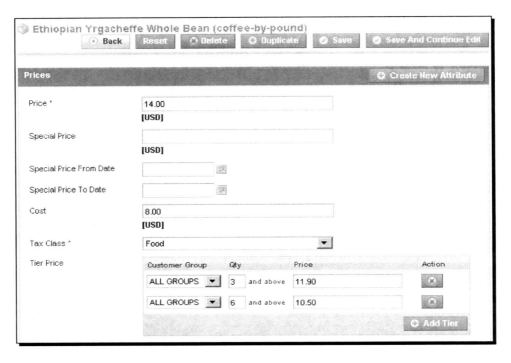

When the product is listed in your catalogue, customers see the standard price and the lowest price. Look at the following screenshot:

On the product's page, customers see the tier prices as shown in the following screenshot:

When you give discounts to only selected groups of customers, the process becomes a little more complex.

Looking ahead: Giving discounts to specified customer groups

As stated earlier, a tiered price has three components. When setting up a tiered price for everyone, we selected **ALL GROUPS** for the **Customer Group**. Magento comes with four in-built customer groups, as shown in the following screenshot:

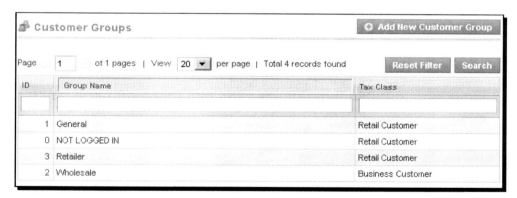

Under **Customers | Customer Groups**, you can create additional customer groups.

With customer groups, you can charge different tax rates for different kinds of customers. In the above screenshot, you can see that one customer group is called **Wholesale**. This group is taxed differently, as you can see from the **Tax Class** column.

You can also give different prices to different customer groups. This is done using the tiered pricing.

A complete discussion of customer groups is beyond the scope of this quick-start guide. However, if you need to offer different prices or tax rates to different types of customers, customer groups enable you to do that.

Pop quiz

1. After you create a Product, which of these cannot be changed?

   a. The Product's type (simple, group, configurable)

   b. The Product's SKU

   c. The Product's name

   d. The Product's Attribute Set

2. Before creating a Configurable Product, you must:

   a. Create all the Simple Products that you will associate with this Configurable Product

   b. Create all the Configurable Attributes and the Attribute Set that you will use for the product

   c. Create the Category that will assign to the product

3. If one of the Simple Products that is associated with a Grouped Product is out of stock, can the customer still add the Grouped Product to their Shopping Cart? (Yes/No)

Summary

In this chapter, we walked through the process of creating a Simple Product, which is the basis for the other product types. We then created a Group Product, which is a collection of Simple Products that is added to a shopper's cart all at once. We also created a Configurable Product. It is a collection of Simple Products that differ in one or more Attributes, and can be chosen one at a time.

Magento contains other product types, which are not covered here. Mastering the creation of Simple Products will enable you to learn about additional product types.

8
Customer Relationships

Magento sends emails to you and your customers under several conditions. Customers receive emails when they create accounts, when they place orders, and when their orders are shipped. The store administrator receives emails when customers fill out the Contact Us form, and sometimes when the store administrator creates an order for a customer (instead of the customer placing the order online).

To make all of these email functions work correctly, you must configure them. In this chapter, we will cover how to configure the most basic and necessary email functions. First, we will cover the basic configuration that is needed for all of these email functions. Next, we will cover the configuration of the **Contact Us** feature, which enables your customers to contact you through a form on your site. Finally, we will learn how to manage customer accounts.

Configuring store email addresses

The email addresses that Magento uses to send and receive emails are set up under **System | Configuration | Store Email Addresses**. Have a look at the following screenshot:

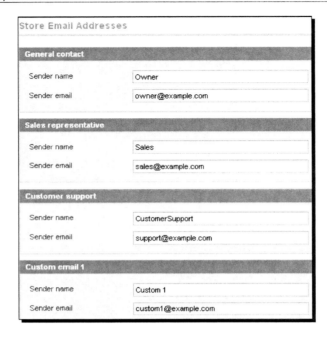

Notice that each of the email addresses has fields labeled **Sender name** and **Sender email**. These are outgoing email addresses. Magento sends emails, but does not receive them. For example, suppose that Magento sends out a customer support email. Even though the email came from Magento, to the customer it will appear to come from the **Customer support** email address and the **Sender name** will be displayed in the email. This helps your customers in two ways.

First, when your customer gets an email from Magento with a **Sender name** such as Brew-Me-A-Cup Customer support, (s)he knows immediately that the message is from your store, and is not spam. Second, if you enter a working email address for the **Sender email**, the customer can just click on *Reply* in his or her email application to reach you.

Time for action: Entering email addresses for your store

Follow these steps to enter email addresses for your store:

1. Go to **System | Configuration | Store Email Addresses**.
2. At a minimum, you should enter the **General contact**, **Sales representative**, and **Customer support** email addresses.
3. Save the page.

What just happened?

The email addresses that you just entered will be used in your store's contact forms. When your customers fill out one of these forms, their message will be sent to the email address(s) that you entered here.

Configuring Contact Us

Magento can give your visitors an online form that they can use to contact you. This can be a better option than posting your email address on your store. Posting your email address makes it vulnerable to being spammed. The address is likely to be harvested by spammers. However, it is more difficult to spam an online form. Also, the online form prompts the customer to enter all of the information that you need to help the customer.

By default, Magento puts a **Contact Us** link at the bottom of each page. This link takes you to a **Contact Us** form at `/index.php/contacts/`.

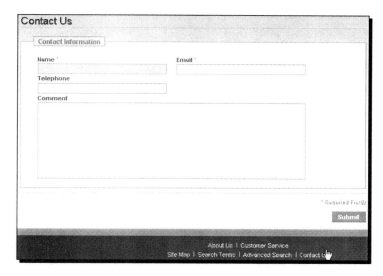

Magento emails the contents of this form to the email address of your choice. You must enter that email address and other configuration options for this form.

You can also disable this form. If you don't use the **Contact Us** function, consider putting your contact information into one of the callouts so that customers are reassured they can reach you.

Time for action: Configuring the Contact Us form

1. Make sure that you have an email address that is set up to receive messages from the contact form. For example, our demo store is at `brew-me-a-cup.com`. We might create an email address `contact@brew-me-a-cup.com` to receive messages from our store's contact form. This was covered in the previous *Time for action* section.

2. From the Admin interface, select **System | Configuration | Contacts**.

3. Expand the **Contact Us** and **Email Options** by clicking on them:

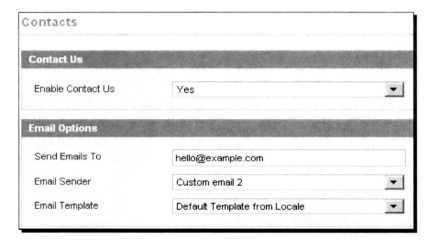

Notice that the **Contact Us** function is enabled by default. Also notice the fictional email address, which you must change.

4. To display a **Contact Us** link at the bottom of each page, for **Enable Contact Us** select **Yes**. Selecting **No** will remove the link.

5. In the field **Send Emails To**, enter the email address that you have set up for receiving messages sent by the contact form. Remember, this is the recipient of the form.

6. In the field **Email Sender**, select one of the email addresses that you set up under **Store Email Addresses**.

7. Modifying email templates is beyond the scope of this quick-start guide. Leave the **Email Template** field set to **Default Template from Locale**.

8. Click on the **Save Config** button.

What just happened?

The **Contact Us** form for your site is now configured. Messages sent using this form will now be sent to and will appear to come from the email address that you configured.

Managing customers

In Magento, a customer is any shopper who has created an account in your store. In this quick-start guide, we differentiate customers from shoppers—customers have accounts, and shoppers are just visitors to your store's site.

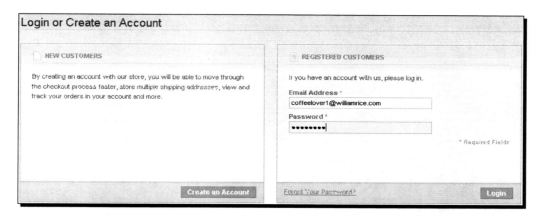

When a customer creates an account, (s)he fills out the new user form. This form doesn't require the customer to fill in personal information, although that can be entered in the customer's profile later:

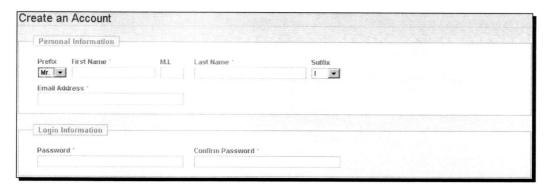

Advantages of having customer accounts

Using customer accounts on your site has advantages for your customers as well as for you. Before we learn how to manage customers, let's discuss some of the advantages.

Advantages for the customer

From the customer's point of view, creating an account in your store has several advantages. For example, a customer can store addresses for billing, shipping, and alternative addresses (such as a work address for taking delivery during the day).

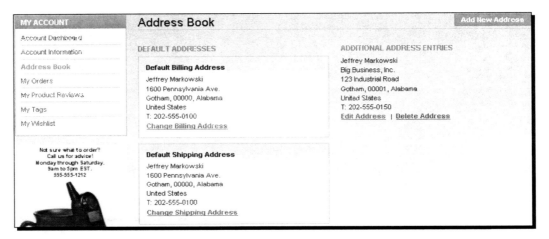

During the checkout process, a customer can select the following addresses that (s)he has stored in the profile, instead of typing them every time (s)he orders:

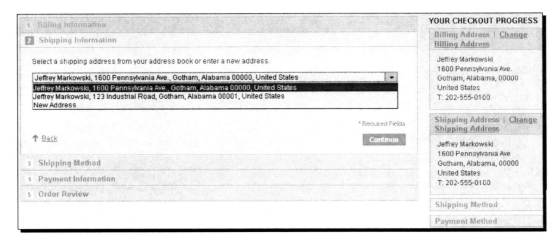

Customers can also track their orders as shown in the following screenshot:

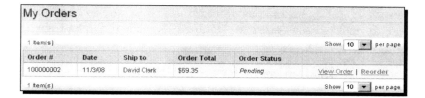

Finally, customers can review and tag Products, and create wish lists.

Advantages for the administrator

From the store administrator's point of view, there are also advantages when your customers create accounts on your site. When a shopper places several orders with your store, you can't guarantee that the shopper will use the same name each time. For example, a customer could use William Rice or Bill Rice. Magento's reports on a customer's history are sorted by the customer's name. If some of your customers have used several names, these reports will not be completely accurate. When a customer uses a name and address that (s)he has stored online, the customer's name will be the same for every order. This enables you to get accurate reports on customer activity, such as the following one under **Reports | Customers**:

Customers can subscribe to your newsletter, which gives you a chance to further build your relationship with them.

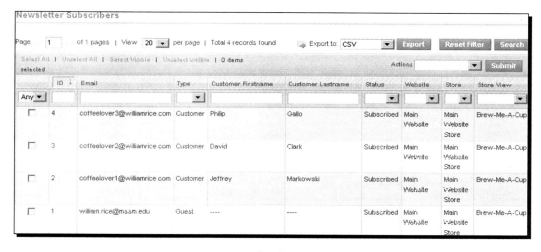

You can organize your customers into Customer Groups. This enables you to assign different price levels and tax rules to each Customer Group, as shown in the following screenshot:

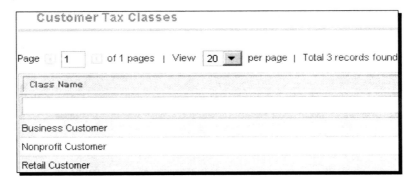

Let's look at how Magento enables you to manage customer accounts and how you can use them.

Time for action: Configuring customer account options

Before using customer accounts, you should configure your customer settings. You do this under **System | Configuration | Customer Configuration**:

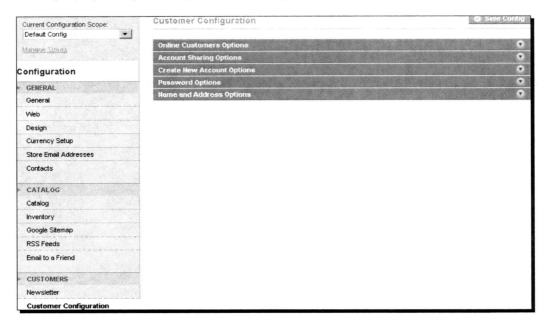

There are five sections under **Customer Configuration**. Let's examine each of them.

1. Online Customers Options

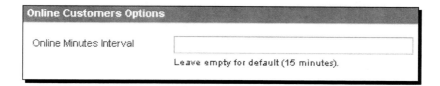

Magento enables you to see which customers are online at any particular time. You can see this by selecting **Customers | Online Customers**.

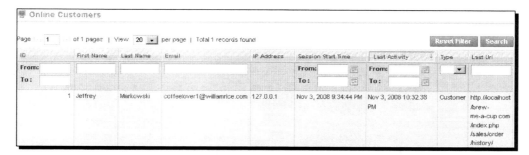

This report is refreshed every few minutes. The time interval is set under **Online Customers Options**.

2. Account Sharing Options

The settings in this section are relevant only if you have created multiple stores on the same site. This quick-start guide only covers creating a single store. As a basic user, you can safely skip this section.

3. Create New Account Options

When your customers create accounts, the options that you set for them will affect how they create those accounts and how you use them. These options are as follows:

- **Default Group**: This is the Customer Group to which every new customer is assigned. For a simple site, you can leave this set to the default of **General**. If you begin using different Customer Groups to classify your customers (business, non-profit, wholesale, and so on), you can assign them to the groups later. For now, you only need to differentiate between shoppers who are not logged in and customers who are logged in. Customers will belong to the group **General**, and all others will belong to **NOT LOGGED IN**.

❏ **Default Email Domain**: When a shopper or customer places an order in your store, (s)he must enter an email address to fill out the order form. After the order is placed, Magento sends a confirmation email to the address that the shopper enters. Magento also enables you to create what is called an **Admin Order**. This is an order that the site administrator (you) enters into the system for the shopper. For example, if you take an order over the phone instead of the shopper using your web site. In that case, you will fill out an order form in the same way that an online shopper would. That order form would also have a place for the shopper's email address. When creating an Admin Order, the shopper might not have an email address. Remember, you are creating an order for someone who cannot or will not use your online form. On an Admin Order, if you leave the shopper's email address blank, Magento will create an email address for the shopper. That email address will be `customer_id@default_email_domain`. For example, if you create an Admin Order for customer ID number 2, and you enter a **Default Email Domain** of **brew-me-a-cup.com**, Magento will send an order confirmation to the email address `2@ brew-me-a-cup.com`. As you can see, the **Default Email Domain** is relevant only if you create Admin Orders, and your customers don't give you an email address to send order confirmations. In that situation, you can use the **Default Email Domain** to have Magento send you a confirmation at your domain for your records.

❏ **Default Welcome Email**: When a user creates a customer account, Magento sends the new customer a welcome email. This field enables you to select the template for that email. You can create new email templates and edit the default templates that come with Magento. Editing these templates is beyond the scope of this book. As a basic Magento user, you can safely leave this set to the default.

❏ **Email Sender**: Select the email address that the recipients (new customers) will see in the "From" field of their welcome email.

❏ **Require Emails Confirmation**: If you select **Yes** for this field, new customers must confirm their accounts by clicking a link in the welcome email. This is an extra step to creating a customer account. You will inevitably lose some people at this step, as some people will consider it too inconvenient. Consider the trade-off. This is extra security for you, but extra inconvenience for your customer.

❑ **Confirmation Link Email** and **Welcome Email**: Use these fields to select the email template for the account confirmation and welcome emails. Modifying email templates is beyond the scope of this quick-start guide. Leave these fields set to **Default Template from Locale**.

4. **Password Options**

These fields determine how a customer can retrieve his or her forgotten password. Leave **Forgot Email Template** set to **Default Template from Locale**. For the field **Forgot Email Sender**, select the email address that customers will see in the "From" field when they receive their password reminder.

5. **Name and Address Options**

This section contains settings for the **Name** and **Address** sections of the new customer form.

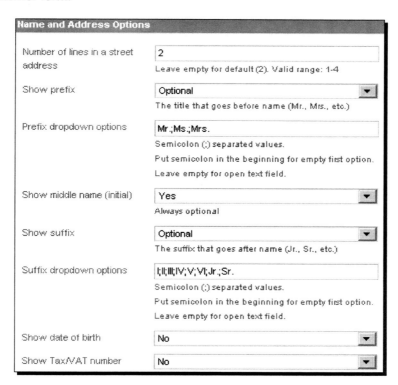

Most of the fields in the configuration screen are self-explanatory. The **Prefix** and **Suffix** fields enable the customer to add a title before and after the name, as you can see in the following form:

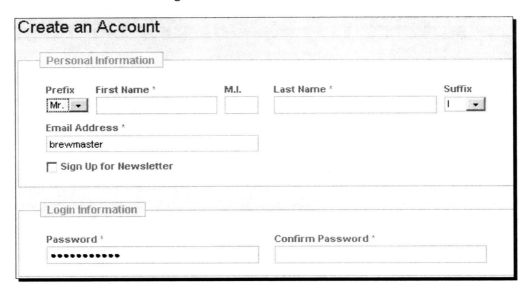

When you finish configuring the new customer function, click on the **Save Config** button. Now you're ready for customers to begin registering and using their accounts.

What just happened?

You customer accounts are configured, and are ready to be used by your customers.

Pop quiz

1. Under **System | Configuration | Store Email Addresses**, the email addresses that you enter are:

    a.   Used by Magento to receive emails from your customers

    b.   Used by Magento to send emails to your customers

    c.   Not used by Magento at all, but are displayed on contact forms for your customers' information

2. In Magento, is the **Contact Us** form enabled by default? Yes/No.

3. Reports about customer activity are found under which menu?

    a.   Sales

    b.   Customers

    c.   Reports

Summary

In this chapter, we examined the advantages of having customer accounts. These advantages apply to both customers and to the store administrator. Then we examined the options that you can set for your customers' accounts. You should encourage your customers to make accounts on your site, and select the settings that make it as easy and quick as possible for them to create those accounts.

9
Accepting Payment

Magento enables you to accept many different kinds of online payments.
This chapter will cover the Checkout and Sales configuration, and the various
payment types supported by Magento. A look at the **System | Configuration**
| Payment Methods *page will show a list of the online payment types that*
Magento supports.

The page looks as follows:

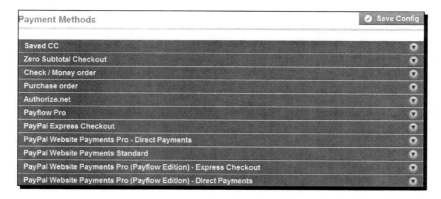

Not shown in this screenshot is Google Checkout, another option for accepting payment. That
is on a separate page. There is also a separate page where you enter your PayPal accounts.

In this chapter, we will look at the details of setting up the different payment types.

Before we cover the topic of accepting payment, we need to perform some configuration.
This is the subject of the next section. Then, we will move on to configuring the payment
methods shown in the previous screenshot.

Checkout and Sales configuration

Various configuration options are scattered around the **System | Configuration** menu, which must be set before you can accept payments. After you set these miscellaneous options, you can proceed to configure Magento to accept credit cards, checks, money orders, and PayPal.

The Sales Tax page

The **System | Configuration | Tax** page contains some configuration options, which you should set before going online with your store. Not all of the options on this page need to be set. We will cover the ones that you must review and/or set.

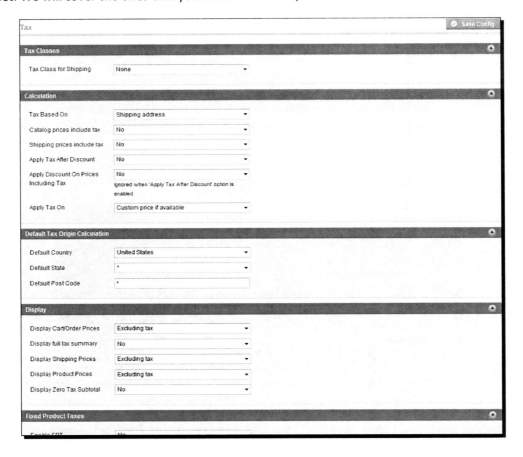

In Chapter 4, we created Tax Classes for our Products. Under **Tax Class for Shipping**, you should set the Tax Class for shipping charges. If you ship to locations that require you to select a sales tax for shipping, then you will probably want to configure the Tax Class labeled **Shipping**, which is built into Magento.

The fields under the **Calculation** section determine when the sales tax is applied. For example, in Chapter 7 we covered *Tiered pricing*, where you give a discount for buying certain quantities. The field **Apply Tax After Discount** determines whether you apply sales tax before or after this discount is applied.

Default Tax Origin Calculation should be set to your business location. If your business is located in one taxing jurisdiction and your products are being shipped from a different jurisdiction, consult a tax adviser about how this affects your tax liability.

Display determines how taxes are displayed in the Shopping Cart. By default, taxes are displayed separately from prices. You can choose to display prices including tax.

Fixed Product Tax always adds the same amount of tax to a product, no matter what price the product is. After enabling the fixed tax, you can add an Attribute to the Product to record the fixed tax. This is useful for items where the jurisdiction charges a flat tax per item. For example, many states charge a flat tax on each automobile tire, to help pay for the disposal of used tires.

The Checkout page

Logged-in users can use a feature called One Page Checkout, which you can enable or disable. One Page Checkout is enabled by default.

The One Page Checkout feature puts all of the checkout items on a single page, in separate tabs. The customer proceeds from tab to tab, but never leaves that page. A sidebar on the right shows the customer's progress, as shown in the following screenshot:

Time for action: Configuring Checkout options

1. Go to **System | Configuration | Sales | Checkout**.

2. Enable or disable the **Allow Guest Checkout** option. This field determines whether someone who has not created an account on your site can complete a purchase. If you set this to **No**, then buyers must create an account while completing their purchases. You should weigh the benefits of making customers create accounts against the chance of losing customers during the checkout, because they may not want to create accounts. By default, this is set to **Yes** so that customers are not required to create accounts to complete a purchase.

3. Set the amount of time for which a shopper can keep an item in his/her Shopping Cart.

4. The field **Quote Lifetime (days)** determines how long a Product can site in a customer's saved Shopping Cart before the price expires. If your prices change every few days, you should set this such that a customer won't have the old price if (s)he returns to a saved Shopping Cart.

5. Determine if a Grouped Product has its own image in the Shopping Cart.

6. Recall that a Grouped Product consists of a group of Simple Products. Also, recall that when a Grouped Product is added to the Shopping Cart, each of the Simple Products is added individually. The field **Grouped product image** determines if the thumbnail image for those individual Products will be the one for the Group, or different for each individual Product.

7. Determine if a Configurable Product has its own image in the Shopping Cart.

8. Recall that a Configurable Product also consists of a group of Simple Products, each one being slightly different. The **Configurable product image** field determines if the thumbnail image for a Configurable Product will be the one for the Configurable Product, or for the individual Simple Product that was chosen.

What just happened?

In the previous procedure, you set some basic options for how your checkout process will work. The most important was whether you will force shoppers to create an account to check out, or allow guests to check out.

The Sales configuration page

The Sales configuration page can be found at **System | Configuration | Sales | Sales**. The configuration options affect the display of the Shopping Cart.

Time for action: Setting the Sales configuration

Follow these steps to set the Sales configuration:

1. Go to **System | Configuration | Sales | Sales**.

2. At a minimum, set these options—**Checkout totals sort order, Allow Reorder, Address**, and **Allow Gift Messages**.

3. The section **Checkout totals sort order** is used to sort out the calculated items that appear in the Shopping Cart. Their normal order is:

   - ❑ **Subtotal**
   - ❑ **Discount**
   - ❑ **Shipping**
   - ❑ **Fixed Product Tax**
   - ❑ **Grand Total**

   Notice that **Tax** is displayed after **Discount**. This makes sense if you're applying the discount first. However, if you set **Apply Tax After Discount** to **No**, that means you're applying the **Tax** first and then the **Discount**. In that case, you might want to use this page to display the **Tax** before the **Discount**.

   Notice also that **Tax** is displayed after **Shipping**. If you know that you will never charge tax on shipping, you could rearrange these and put **Shipping** after **Tax**. That would make it clear to the customer that you are calculating **Tax** before **Shipping**. Therefore, there is no tax on shipping.

4. **Allow Reorder** saves a copy of the past orders in a customer's account. The customer can then just click on the saved copy to duplicate that order.

If your inventory changes often, you might want to disable this. You don't want customers to try to **Reorder** items that are no longer available, or imply that they can do this when they can't.

5. Under **Invoice and Packing Slip Design**, remember to enter your business address. While this is not required by Magento, imagine receiving a gift that someone else sent from a store with a packing slip that has no contact information for the business that sent it. You can also enter your business phone number and email here, so that the recipient of an item from your store has all of your contact information.

6. The **Gift Messages** section determines if a customer can add a gift message for the order, and/or for individual items in the order.

7. Save your settings.

What just happened?

The settings configured in the previous section will affect the look and function of the checkout process for your customers.

The General configuration page

By default, Magento is configured for the United States. If you are not located in the Eastern United States, you should change the settings on the **General** configuration page. It can be found at **System | Configuration | General | General**, and looks as follows:

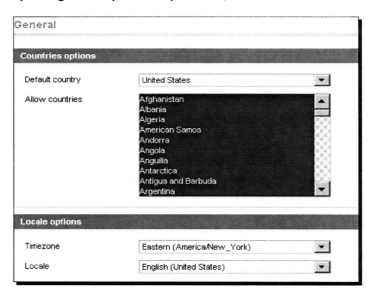

Currency Setup page

The **Currency Setup** page is used to set the currencies that will be used in your Magento store. We can also select the currencies that will be allowed in the store.

Time for action: Configuring Magento for your location and currency

1. Go to **System | Configuration | General** and configure Magento for your location.

2. Go to **System | Configuration | Currency Setup**.

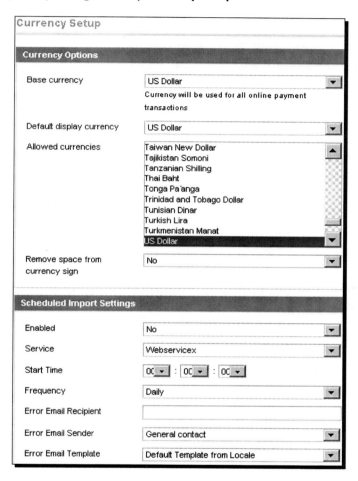

3. The **Base currency** is the currency that will be used for the backend of your store. The **Default display currency** is the currency that the customers will see in your catalog. For example, if you are in the UK and you are selling to customers in the US, your **Base currency** would be **British Pound Sterling** and your **display currency** would be **US Dollar**.

4. **Allowed currencies** determines which currency or currencies your customers can choose.

5. If you allow only one currency, then the drop-down menu that enables customers to choose currencies will be hidden.

6. If you allow customers to select different currencies, or if you have a different **Base currency** and **Default display currency**, you should set up currency exchange rates under **Scheduled Import Settings**. This will update the exchange rates daily, enabling Magento to convert between currencies.

7. If you want to use a currency that is not shown in this list, it is probably because that currency is not installed. Go to **Advanced | System** and select the **Currency** section. You will see a list of the **Installed Currencies**. If the currency you want to use is not selected, then select it and save the configuration.

What just happened?

Magento is ready to be configured for online payment methods.

You are now ready to configure your payment methods. Let's begin with an overview of the online payment process for credit cards. Next, we will cover the details of each of the payment methods.

An overview of the online payment process for credit cards

To process credit cards online, the following four components need to work together:

1. Shopping Cart.
2. Payment Gateway.
3. Merchant Account.
4. Bank Account.

Each of these components does a specific job in the order presented here. In the following subsections, we will discuss each component.

Shopping Cart

Like most e-commerce systems, Magento uses a Shopping Cart to hold the customer's items. In addition to the items that the customer is buying, the Shopping Cart also holds the amount that the customer owes.

Magento's Shopping Cart is built-in; you don't need to use a separate piece of software to create a Shopping Cart.

Payment Gateway

When a customer proceeds to the checkout screen, (s)he chooses the payment method. If a customer chooses to pay by credit card, (s)he must then enter the credit card details. When the customer clicks on the **Submit** button and sends the credit card information, a piece of software called the Payment Gateway takes over. The **Payment Gateway** is the equivalent of the physical credit card terminal located in most retail outlets.

The Payment Gateway securely transmits the credit card information to the credit card network, such Visa or MasterCard. The network validates the credit card information and amount. That is, Visa, MasterCard, or some other network determines that the credit card is valid and has the funds available. The network gives the transaction an authorization number, which the Gateway returns to Magento. Thus, the payment is authorized.

You should keep in mind that the Payment Gateway is both a piece of software and a service. The software communicates between your Shopping Cart and the credit card network. The service performs the card validation. The software part of the Payment Gateway is built into Magento; the service isn't. You will need to open an account with one of the Payment Gateways that Magento supports.

Merchant Account and business Bank Account

After the credit card payment is authorized, the money must be transferred from the credit card account to your business's checking account. This is done by the **Merchant Account**.

A Merchant Account is more than just another bank account. It is an account, a contract with the credit card network(s) from which you will accept payment, and also a line of credit. All of these features together form a Merchant Account.

The credit card network transfers money from the credit card account to the Merchant Account. If you have a Merchant Account, it is the end of the process. You can then choose to keep the money in your Merchant Account, or transfer it to another Bank Account.

Opening a Merchant Account can be expensive. It requires a credit check, and in some cases, collateral. Also, there is a monthly maintenance fee that is higher than a normal bank account. However, there is a way for you to accept credit card payments without a Merchant Account. We will deal with that in the next section. The following image shows the complete process:

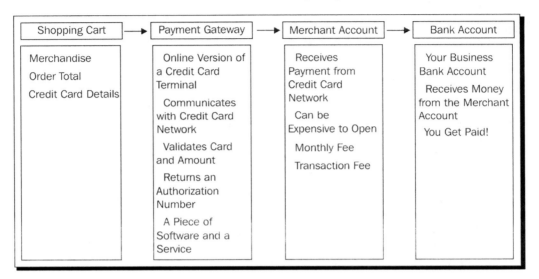

Where do PayPal, Authorize.net, and Payflow fit in?

The previous section explained the following four components of the credit card process:

1. Shopping Cart.
2. Payment Gateway.
3. Merchant Account.
4. Bank Account.

In Magento, the Shopping Cart is a built-in feature, you only need to configure it, and the Bank Account is yours. That means you still need a Payment Gateway and Merchant Account. PayPal, Authorize.net, and Payflow can perform these functions.

Payflow Pro is a Payment Gateway

Payflow Pro is a Payment Gateway. If you have your own Merchant Account, you can use Payflow Pro to validate credit card payments.

To use Payflow Pro, you must open a Payflow Pro account. As of this writing, Payflow is owned by PayPal. So, you would need to go to the PayPal web site, `www.PayPal.com`, to open a Payflow account.

If you use Payflow Pro, the process looks as follows:

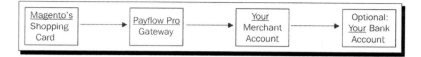

Notice that a Bank Account is optional because you own the Merchant Account. Since the funds are transferred from the credit card network into your Merchant Account, you now have the money. It is your decision to keep it in your Merchant Account or transfer it to a Bank Account.

PayPal and Authorize.net are Gateways plus Merchant Accounts

If you do not have or do not want a Merchant Account, you can still use PayPal and Authorize.net to process credit card transactions. When these companies process a credit card transaction for you, they act as both the Payment Gateway and the Merchant Account. This means that you don't need to open a separate Merchant Account. Instead, PayPal and Authorize.net will:

1.   Validate the credit card transaction.

2.   Accept funds from the credit card network.

3.   Transfer those funds to your Bank Account.

If you use PayPal or Authorize.net, the process looks as follows:

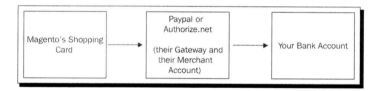

Notice that a Bank Account is required. That is because PayPal or Authorize.net must transfer the funds from their Merchant Account to your Bank Account.

Which option is the best for credit card processing?

So far, we looked at three options for credit card processing: PayPal, Authorize.net, and Payflow Pro. Now you need to decide which is the best for your business.

If your store has two hundred or more transactions a month, consider using Payflow Pro. You will need to open and maintain your own Merchant Account, which is an added expense. However, the fee for each transaction is usually smaller than PayPal and Authorize.net (because Payflow does less, as it's only a Gateway). Also, Payflow has better reporting tools.

If you have a physical store and are adding an online store, you probably already have a Merchant Account. In that case, Payflow Pro will probably be your best option for processing credit cards.

If you want to accept both credit cards and regular PayPal payments, then PayPal is the obvious choice. Magento can be configured to accept both credit card and email-based payments from PayPal.

If you have a low volume of sales, or don't have the fee, or a good enough credit rating to open a Merchant Account, consider either PayPal or Authorize.net.

Payment methods in detail

The following sections describe each of the payment methods available in Magento. These methods are available on the **System | Configuration | Payment Methods** page, and also on Google Checkout. The payment methods in Magento can be seen in the following screenshot:

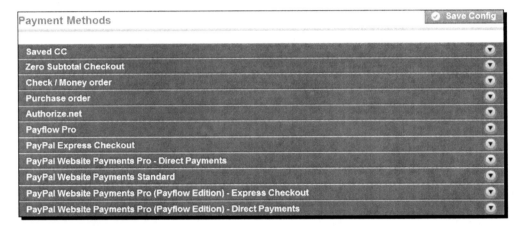

Remember that to use any of the PayPal methods, you must enrol in PayPal and enter your PayPal account information under **System | Configuration | PayPal Accounts**.

The following subsections give you details about each of the payment methods available in Magento. However, no step-by-step directions of how to set up each payment method are given. This is for two reasons. First, the official Magento site contains thorough directions for configuring each of these payment methods. Second, some of these configuration options are likely to change while this book is in print.

 Instead of telling you how to configure each payment method, the following sections focus on a more difficult task. They give you the information you need to decide which payment methods are best for your store, and what effect each method might have on your business.

Use this information to select the payment methods that are best for your business. Then, head to the official Magento site for directions on how to configure them.

Saved CC

When you enable this payment method, Magento will save the customer's credit card information along with the order. Offline, you can verify the credit card payment.

If you have a physical store where you already accept credit cards, you could use this method. You could use Magento to capture and save the credit card information, and process the payment information later. This would require you to manually process each order.

If you already have a Merchant Account for your physical store, and you expect your online sales volume to be low, then this is a quick and free way to accept credit card payments online.

To use this method, you need a Merchant Account and a credit card terminal.

Zero Subtotal Checkout

If you enable this method, when a customer places an order and the product total is equal to zero, the customer will not be asked to enter any payment information. You might use this if you offer free samples from your store.

Check/Money Order

When you enable this payment method, and the customer selects it during checkout, the customer is given your payment address and the **Make Check payable to** information, as shown in the following screenshot:

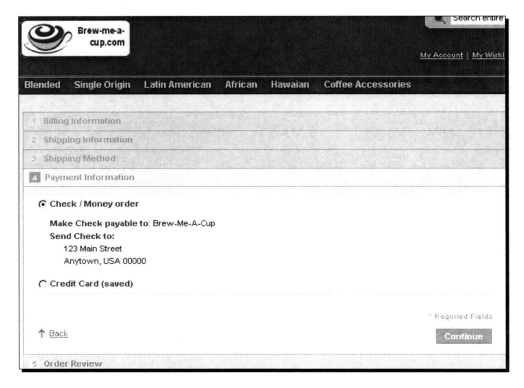

To use this method, you only need a bank account where you can deposit checks and money orders.

Purchase Order

When you enable this payment method, and the customer selects it during checkout, Magento prompts the customer to enter the purchase order number. This purchase order number will appear on the order that is submitted to your store.

This is an offline payment method, like Check/Money Order and Saved Credit Card. You must manually check the purchase order number that the customer entered against your records. This means that you are maintaining purchase order numbers in a system outside of Magento.

To use this method, you need a system for tracking purchase orders and a bank account.

Authorize.net

If you enable this method, customers can enter their credit card information just as they do on any e-commerce site. There is no indication that Authorize.net is processing the credit card. The customer remains on your site while Authorize.net processes the credit card.

To use this method, you need to enrol in `www.authorize.net`, and should have a bank account.

Payflow Pro

If this method is enabled, customers can enter their credit card information just as they do on any e-commerce site. There is no indication that Payflow is processing the credit card. The customer remains on your site while Payflow processes the credit card.

To use this method, you need to enrol in Payflow Pro and should have a Merchant Account.

PayPal Express Checkout

This is the traditional PayPal method, where no credit card is needed. Instead, money is transferred from the buyer's PayPal account to the seller's PayPal account.

 Your customer needs a PayPal account to use the **PayPal Express Checkout** method.

If a customer is shipping an order to multiple addresses, (s)he cannot select this payment method.

When the customer selects this method, (s)he will be redirected to the PayPal web site.

After selecting **PayPal Express** or **PayPal Standard** as the payment method, the customer continues to the **Order Review** step, where (s)he confirms the order.

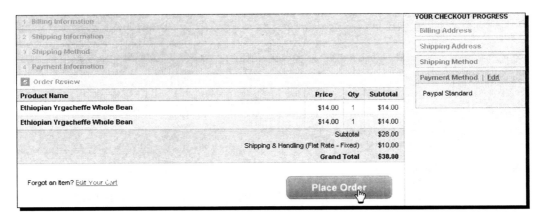

After clicking on the **Place Order** button, the customer is taken to the PayPal site shown in the following screenshot:

Then, the customer sees your store as the payee, and the amount to be paid. The customer also chooses a shipping address.

The customer then authorizes the payment. Money is transferred from the buyer's PayPal account to your PayPal account.

After the payment is done, the buyer is taken back to your store. The merchandise is shipped to the address that the buyer has on file at PayPal. The shipping address that the buyer entered into Magento is ignored.

The completed order displays the shipping address that Magento received from PayPal. The billing address section is empty.

PayPal Website Payments Standard

The processing flow for **PayPal Standard** is almost identical to **PayPal Express**. That is, the customer will be temporarily taken off your site and to the PayPal site to submit their payment.

The only differences are that the shipping address from Magento is used instead of the shipping address from the customer's PayPal account, and PayPal Standard allows credit cards.

To use PayPal Express or Standard, you just need a PayPal account and a bank account. PayPal Standard is probably the easiest way to accept credit card payments on your site. The only disadvantage is that customers leave your site during the checkout process, which might result in a greater number of abandoned transactions.

PayPal Website Payments Pro—Direct Payments

If you enable this method, customers can enter their credit card information just as they do on any e-commerce site. There is no indication that PayPal is processing the credit card. The customer remains on your site while PayPal processes the credit card.

To use this method, you just need a PayPal account and a bank account. As of this writing, if you select this method, PayPal requires that you also offer your customers PayPal Express checkout. That is, if you have PayPal process your credit cards, you must also offer your customers the option of using their PayPal account.

This is probably the most professional-looking option for processing credit cards, because customers don't leave your site to submit payment. However, you might want to reassure customers that their credit cards are safe by putting a notice on your payment page like, "Your credit card is processed by PayPal, an established leader in e-commerce safety and security!"

PayPal Website Payments Pro (Payflow Edition)—Express and Direct

With the previous four PayPal methods, PayPal is both our payment gateway and your merchant account. That is, PayPal processes the credit card, and, accepts the money from the credit card company and transfers it into your account. If you use the **Payflow** method, then PayPal becomes only your payment gateway. That is, PayPal will only process the credit card payments. They will not act as your merchant account. You will need to establish a merchant account elsewhere, and link **PayPal Payflow** to that account. This might be a good option for you if you have a physical store that accepts credit cards, and you are happy with your merchant account. **Payflow** will enable you to accept credit cards online while using the same merchant account that you have been using for your physical store.

Google Checkout

Google Checkout is configured under **System | Configuration | Sales | Google API**. First, let's look at the customer experience when you use this payment method. Then, let's discuss how to decide if it's right for your store.

When you enable Google Checkout, Magento will display a **Google Checkout** button in the customer's **Shopping Cart** as shown in the following screenshot:

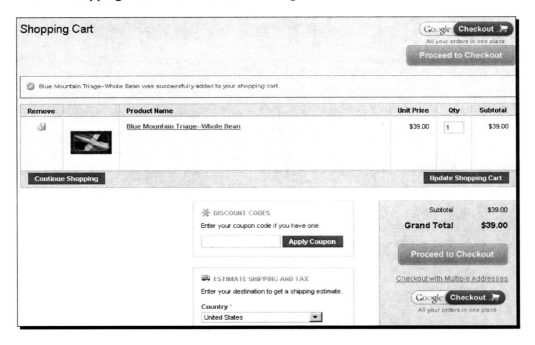

When a customer clicks on the **Google Checkout** button, (s)he is taken to Google's checkout interface. This is completely separate from Magento's checkout process. At this point, the customer must either log into his or her Google account, or create a Google account.

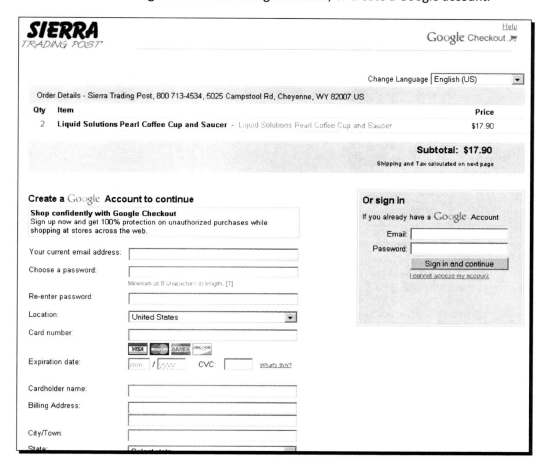

After your customer logs into or creates his/her Google account, Google Checkout displays its own version of a Checkout Page as shown in the following screenshot:

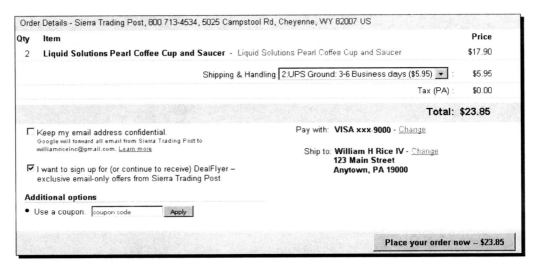

Notice that customers can select the shipping method. The choices on this drop-down menu are carried over from Magento. They are configured in the Google API tab.

Also notice that Google Checkout calculates the sales tax. The tax rules are also carried over from Magento.

The credit card is entered in Google Checkout, not Magento.

You can see that the items in this Shopping Cart were also carried over from Magento. Customers cannot change these items from this screen. To change the items, customers must close this page, return to Magento, and start over.

When a customer clicks the **Place your order now** button, the order is placed. The customer will be returned to Magento.

Unseen by the customer, Google keeps a record of the order in your Google Seller's Account. Google also sends the order information to Magento. Magento will create the order under **Sales | Orders**, where it will be stored with all of the orders that were processed in Magento.

Advantages and disadvantages of Google Checkout

Knowing the advantages and disadvantages of Google Checkout will help you decide if you want to offer it to your customers.

As you can see from the previous subsection, when your customer uses Google Checkout, (s)he is taken from your site to the Google's Checkout site. If the customer doesn't have a Google account, (s)he must create one. This is an extra step for your customer. You might lose some customers during checkout because of the time they must take to create Google accounts.

Another disadvantage of Google Checkout is that it is not as easy to set up in Magento as the other payment methods. The official Magento site has step-by-step directions. However, it is more complicated than the setup for other payment methods.

Google Checkout is available only to customers in the United States.

The last disadvantage to using Google Checkout is that the customer can choose to not give you a telephone number, and can mask his or her email address. This makes it more difficult for you to contact the customer if there's a problem with the order. While Google will forward your email to the customer, you will not know for sure if your message reached the customer and you cannot call the customer to check.

There are several advantages to using Google Checkout. One is that the Google brand might reassure your shoppers that you are legitimate and that their transaction is secure.

Another advantage is that, as of this writing, the transaction fee for Google Checkout is usually lower than that for PayPal or Authorize.net.

Finally, as of this writing, for every $10 that you process through Google Checkout you get a $1 credit with Google Adwords.

Configuring a payment method

Select a payment method and configure it in your store. The easiest payment method to set up is Check/Money Order. Once you have a payment method, you can go through the complete checkout process as a customer.

You should go through the descriptions of the payment methods that we saw, and select the one that best fits the needs of your customers and your business. Select the methods that you want, and then go the official Magento site and search for directions on how to configure them.

Summary

In this chapter, you performed some miscellaneous configuration needed to enable you to accept payments. Then, we discussed the details of various payment methods. By now, you should have a good idea of which payment methods are best for your business. We end the chapter with an assignment: select and configure the payment methods that best meet your needs.

10

Configure Shipping

This chapter covers the configuration of Magento's shipping options. The most difficult part of configuring Magento's shipping options is not performing the actual configuration, but deciding which options are the best for your store. You need to understand how each of the shipping options in Magento affects your finances and your customers' experience. After you decide which shipping options are the best for your store, you need to configure them. Most of the configuration options are self-explanatory.

This chapter will give you the information you need to decide which shipping options are best for you. Next, it will cover the configuration settings that are less obvious, or whose names might be misleading.

Decisions you must make

To help you decide which shipping methods are best for your business, consider the questions discussed in the subsections that follow. Each of these questions equates to a configuration option in Magento. When you know the answer to a question, you can follow through by setting the corresponding configuration option.

Will you allow multiple addresses?

You can allow customers to send the items in their orders to multiple addresses. If you enable this, Magento displays a link in the **Shopping Cart** to **Checkout with Multiple Addresses** as shown in the following screenshot:

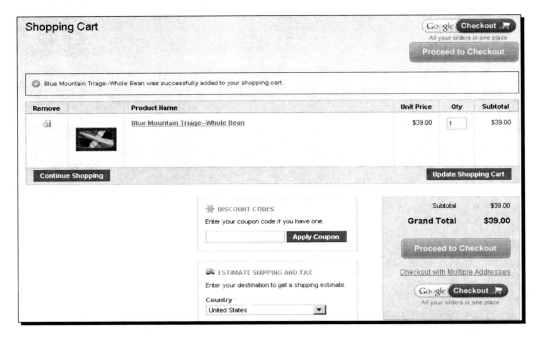

This option is set under **System | Configuration | Shipping Settings | Options**. When a customer chooses this, each item in the **Shopping Cart** can have its own shipping address. If there are two items in the cart, Magento creates two shipping addresses. If there are 20 line items, Magento creates 20 addresses.

If your customer has too many items in the Shopping Cart, and selects **Checkout with Multiple Addresses**, Magento can create so many shipping addresses that it will overwhelm your server. To avoid this, use the **Maximum qty allowed for Shipping to multiple addresses** setting to limit the number of addresses that can be created. This setting is also under **System | Configuration | Shipping Settings | Options**.

What shipping methods will you offer?

Magento enables you to offer your customers a choice of shippers: UPS, FedEx, DHL, and United States Postal Service. Or, you can forgo offering your customers different shippers and just offer them different shipping methods instead such as Flat Rate, or a Shipping Table.

Flat Rate shipping

The Flat Rate method means you add the same shipping charge to every order, no matter how small or large the order is. Think of the Flat Rate as your handling fee. When an order uses this shipping method, the customer does not choose the shipper.

If you use the Flat Rate shipping method, make sure that the sum of the Product's price and the flat rate will cover your cost for packing and shipping the Product.

Table Rate method

The Table Rate method calculates the shipping charge using a table that you create. This table calculates the shipping charge based upon one of the following:

- ◆ Destination and weight
- ◆ Destination and price
- ◆ Destination and the number of items in the order

For example, the following is the shipping rate table for our demo site, which we will create later in this chapter. Notice that the shipping charge is based on destination and price. Also, notice that we have entered a wildcard (*) for the destination, so these shipping charges apply to all destinations. Effectively, we are basing the shipping charge on just the price.

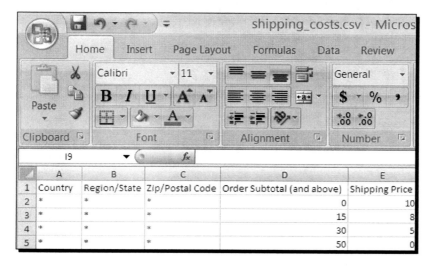

During checkout, your customer will see the shipping charge under the **Shipping Method** section. The subtotal for this order is $39.00, which according to the table in the previous screenshot has a shipping charge of **$5.00**:

When you use the Table Rate method for shipping, you can also add a handling charge. The handling charge will be added to the rate from the table, so that the customer won't see the handling charge as a separate item.

UPS, USPS, FedEx, and DHL

You can offer your customers one or more of the following shippers:

◆ United Parcel Service (UPS)

◆ United States Postal Service (USPS)

◆ Federal Express (FedEx)

◆ DHL

For each shipper that you offer, you can designate which services you make available. You do not need to offer all of the services that the shipper offers.

Offering multiple shipping methods

You can offer your customers none, one, or several of the shippers we just saw.

Note that you do not need to offer your customers a choice of shippers. Using the Table Rate method, you can just offer them a choice of shipping methods instead—such as "5-7 day," "2-day," and "Overnight"—and use the shipper that you think is best for that method. In the following screenshot, we use the Table Rate method to offer the customers **5-7 Day Shipping**, and UPS for **2-day and Overnight** shipping:

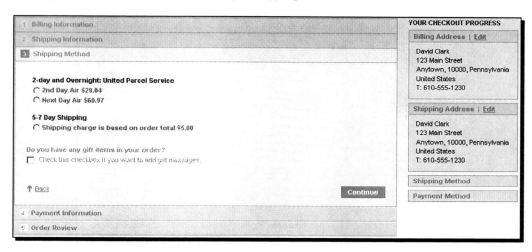

Where can the buyer send the items to?

There are two places in the **Configuration** page where you can designate the countries to which you will ship. First, you set the default **Allow Countries** under **System | Configuration | General** as shown in the following screenshot:

To select multiple countries, hold down the *Ctrl* key while clicking on each country.

Second, you can designate which countries will work with each of the shipping methods that you implement. The choices that you make for each shipping method will override the default that you set under **System | Configuration | General**. In the following example, we are offering **Flat Rate** shipping only to the **United States**. If the shipping address is outside of the **United States**, this method will not be offered.

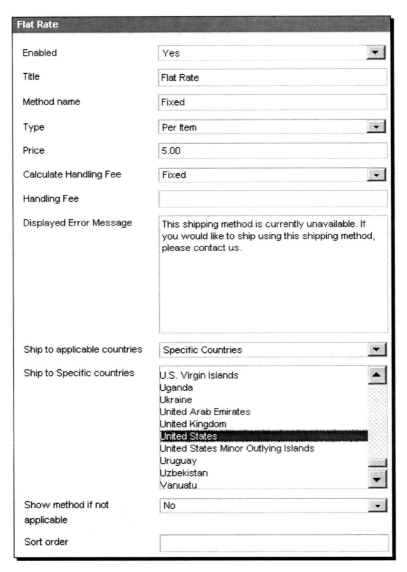

Will you charge a handling fee?

For each of the shipping methods except for Flat Rate, you can add a handling fee. Magento adds this fee to the shipping rate that it gets from the Shipping Table or from the shipper. Your customer will not see the handling fee as a separate charge.

The handling fee is configured separately for each shipping method. The following is an example of adding a **Handling fee** to the rates for UPS:

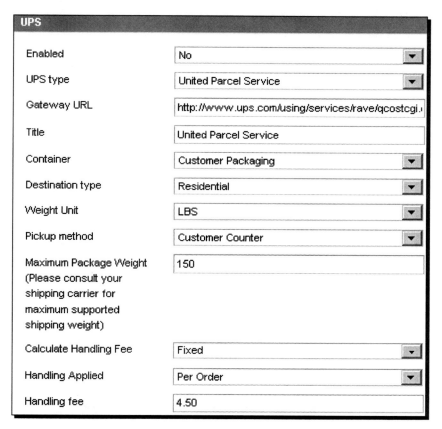

Do you offer free shipping for a minimum dollar amount?

Free Shipping is a separate shipping method. To enable this, go to **System | Configuration | Shipping Methods | Free Shipping**, enter a **Minimum order amount**, and select the countries to which you will ship for free:

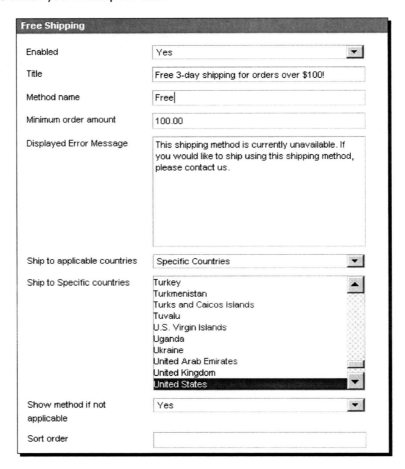

If the order doesn't meet the minimum amount, this shipping method will not be displayed.

Notice the field **Show method if not applicable**. This setting appears only if you previously selected **Specific countries** in the **Ship to applicable counties** field. If you selected **All Allowed Countries**, then this setting is hidden.

By default, this is set to **No**. If the order meets the minimum, but it's not available for the shipping address, this shipping method doesn't display. However, selecting **Yes** for this field displays the Free Shipping method if the order meets the minimum amount, but the country doesn't qualify. In that case, the customer gets the **Displayed Error Message**.

Configuration settings and issues

Now that you have decided what kind of shipping you will offer and what you will charge for shipping, you are ready to configure the shipping method. This section contains the overall configuration settings, plus specific configuration issues for each of the shipping methods.

Time for action: Setting the overall configuration settings that affect shipping

At a minimum, you should set the configuration options in this section before configuring any specific shipping methods.

Select countries to which you will ship

1. Select **System | Configuration | General**.

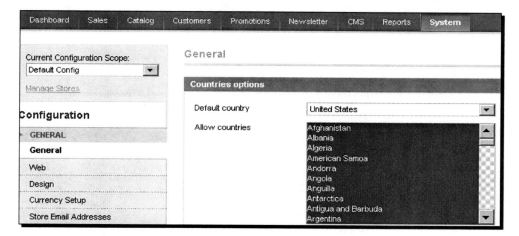

2. For **Default country**, select the default country for shipping addresses.

3. Under **Allow countries**, select all the countries to which you will ship. To select multiple countries, hold down the *Ctrl* key while clicking on each country.

4. Click on the **Save Config** button.

Set the shipping origin and multiple address options

1. Select **System | Configuration | Shipping Settings**:

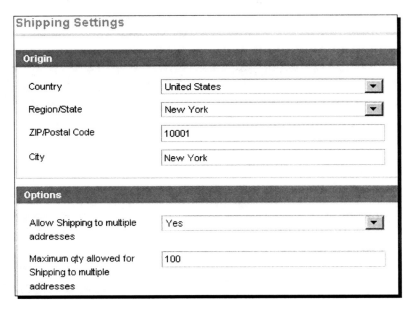

2. Under the **Origin** section, enter the information for where the shipments originate. When Magento contacts the shippers, it will use this information to calculate the shipping charges.

3. Under the **Options** section, determine if you will allow customers to ship each item to a different address, and enter the maximum number of items that you will ship separately.

4. Click on the **Save Config** button.

What just happened?

The general configuration options for shipping have been set. You are ready to configure individual shipping methods.

Configuring Flat Rate shipping

Like all other shipping methods except Free Shipping, the Flat Rate method enables you to enter a handling fee. Go to **System | Configuration | Shipping Settings | Flat Rate**. The handling fee can be a **Fixed** amount or a **Percent** of the order total, as shown in the following screenshot:

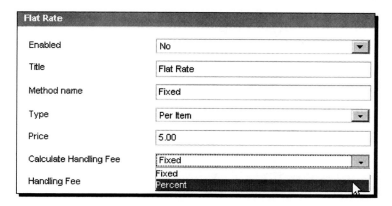

If you enter a fixed handling fee, it will be added to the price, and the shipping charge will be the same every time this method is used. If you enter a percentage for the handling fee, the system will calculate the handling fee based on the order total and add that to the shipping price.

Configure the Table Rate

As stated earlier, the Table Rate method calculates the shipping charge based upon one of the following:

- Destination and weight
- Destination and price
- Destination and number of items in the order

The table of rates is created in Excel (or some other spreadsheet program), saved as a text file, and then uploaded to Magento.

Time for action: Creating a shipping rate table

1. Under **System | Configuration**, look in the upper-left corner. If the **Current Configuration Scope** reads **Default Configuration**, you must change this. This is unique to the Table Rate shipping method. From the drop-down list, select **Main Website** as shown here:

This is necessary because each table of shipping rates applies to only one store. This beginner's guide covers using Magento for only a single store; multiple stores are beyond the scope of this book. For now, just select the store that you are working with.

2. Go to **System | Configuration | Shipping Methods**. Under **Table Rates**, select the **Condition** for calculating shipping rates as shown in the following screenshot:

3. Click on the **Export CSV** button. If the button is not available, then you did not complete step 1 of these directions.

4. Magento will download a file named `tablerates.csv` to your computer. If you do not have a spreadsheet program installed, you can just save the file to your hard drive. But if you do have a spreadsheet program, it will probably offer to open the file for you as shown in this screenshot.

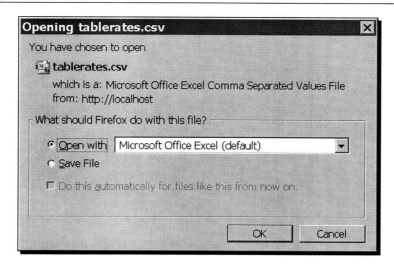

5. Open the file in a spreadsheet program.

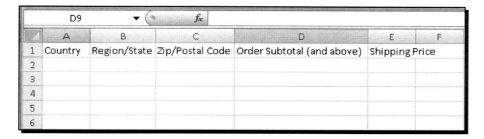

6. The file that you downloaded is created specifically for the **Condition** that you selected. In this example, notice that our **Condition** was **Price vs. Destination**, and this file contains fields for the destination (**Country, Region/State, Zip/Postal Code**) and the price (**Order Subtotal**).

7. Enter the conditions and shipping prices, and then save the file as `shipping_costs.csv`.

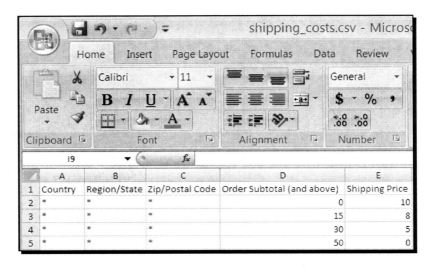

	A	B	C	D	E
1	Country	Region/State	Zip/Postal Code	Order Subtotal (and above)	Shipping Price
2	*	*	*	0	10
3	*	*	*	15	8
4	*	*	*	30	5
5	*	*	*	50	0

8. Next to **Import**, click on the **Browse...** button. A dialog box will open, where you select the file you just created.

9. Select the file with the shipping rates, and click on the **OK** or **Open** button.

10. Click on the **Save Config** button.

11. Fill out the rest of the configuration fields for this shipping method, and save again.

12. Under **System | Configuration**, in the upper-left corner, change **Current Configuration Scope** back to **Default Configuration**.

What just happened?

When we configured the Flat Rate shipping method, we first selected the specific store to which the rates will apply. Next, we exported a blank template for the shipping rates. We opened the template in a spreadsheet program, added our rates, and saved it as a text file. We then imported the completed rates. Finally, we set the configuration scope back to the default. The result is that now Magento holds a table of shipping rates that we created.

Configuring Free Shipping

The Free Shipping method will appear only if the shipping address is in one of the allowed countries and the order total meets the minimum requirement. Even if the order qualifies for free shipping, the customer must still click and select this shipping method. Remember that the customer will see the **Title** that you enter, so make it something more descriptive than just **Free Shipping**. In our demo store, we changed the **Title** to explain why we offer free shipping by going to **System | Configuration | Shipping Methods | Free Shipping.** Look at this screenshot:

UPS

Unlike the other shippers, UPS enables you to choose a **Weight Unit** of pounds or kilograms. All other shippers use the default unit for your store.

Also, unlike the other shippers, you do not need to register for an account with UPS to use their gateway. This makes UPS the easiest shipper to set up.

USPS

To use USPS, you must register for a USPS web tools user ID. At the time of this writing, the URL to register is `https://secure.shippingapis.com/Registration/`. Or, go to `http://www.usps.com/webtools/` and select the link to **Register now to begin using the USPS Web Tools**.

Your new account will work on their testing server. The gateway URL for the testing server is different than the default that is programmed into Magento. Enter the URL for the testing server, test it, and if it works follow the instructions in the email they sent to get your account activated for the production server.

For some users, the test server never works. These users ask to be moved to production right away and, usually, the gateway works for them.

Make sure that your product weight is in ounces and pounds, and that each product has a weight of at least one ounce. Otherwise, the USPS gateway will fail to return any shipping rates at all.

FedEx

To use the FedEx gateway, you must have an Account ID. This is a "production key" that FedEx will give you when you register.

To get a production key, you must register with the FedEx Developer Resource Center. On the FedEx web site, perform a search to locate this page. Then, select the link to **Obtain Production Key** and follow the instructions that are online.

When FedEx supplies you with the production key, enter it into the **Account ID** field in **System | Configuration | Shipping Methods | FedEx**.

DHL

As with USPS and FedEx, DHL requires you to create an account before you can use its gateway. While Magento does have a place to configure DHL, at this time, Magento is not on DHL's list of supported software. This means that while the Magento community will help you troubleshoot DHL configuration, DHL will not help you. You can see the list of Shopping Carts that DHL supports at `http://www.dhl-usa.com/xml/vendormodule.asp?nav=TechnologyTools`.

Time for action: Configuring and testing the shipping rates

Even if you're not sure which shipping options you want to use in your store, at this point you should configure at least one of them. This will enable you to test the full functionality of your Shopping Cart, and place test orders.

1. Configure at least one shipping option and step through the checkout process with that option enabled. This will allow you to see the complete checkout process. The easiest to configure is flat rate shipping.

2. Also, consider which shipper(s) you want to offer, and sign up for accounts with those shippers. When you have your accounts, you can configure Magento to connect to those shippers.

What just happened?

We configured the shipping options for our store. We are now ready to place test orders, which will be covered in the next chapter.

Pop quiz

1. When you offer a shipper, you must offer all of that shipper's services to your customers. True/False

2. When you offer a shipper, you must offer all of the countries to which that company ships. True/False

3. You can add a handling fee for each of the shipping methods, except for (select one):

    a.   Free

    b.   Flat Rate

    c.   Table Rates

    d.   UPS

    e.   USPS

    f.   FedEx

    g.   DHL

4. Which shipper does not require you to register an account, to use its gateway (select one)?

    a.   UPS

    b.   USPS

    c.   FedEx

    d.   DHL

Summary

Magento offers relatively easy ways of configuring shipping options for your customers. All of the methods covered in this chapter have one thing in common: They add a shipping/handling charge to the customer's order, but do not interface directly with a scale, a label printer, or a postage printer. That is, after these methods calculate shipping/handling and add that amount to the order, their job is done. You must still perform these functions in a system outside of Magento.

When you offer your customers a choice of shipping methods, try to use labels that tell your customers what they can expect from a method before selecting it. For example, if you're using FedEx only for overnight shipping, instead of labelling it as "FedEx," label the method "Overnight with FedEx".

Beware of times when the shipping charge that you calculate might not cover your cost of shipping an object. For example, if you're calculating shipping based on weight and destination, and you sell an object that is very light but very bulky (like a paper chandelier), the standard shipping cost for that item's weight might not cover your cost. So, keep unusual shipping costs in mind when pricing your products.

11
Fulfilling an Order

In Magento, fulfilling an order usually follows a logical order of steps. Magento has features that you can use at each step of an order's lifecycle. While these features are not perfect, they are impressive and easy to use.

In this chapter we will see the lifecycle of an order, and certain tips for managing orders. Next, we will practice the processing of an order.

The lifecycle of an order

This section will walk you through the process of fulfilling an order. At each step of the process, we will discuss the features that Magento offers for that step.

Step 1: Customer places the order

After a customer places an order on your site, both you and the customer will see the status of the order as either **Pending** or **Processing**. Your customer will see this after clicking on the **My Account** link.

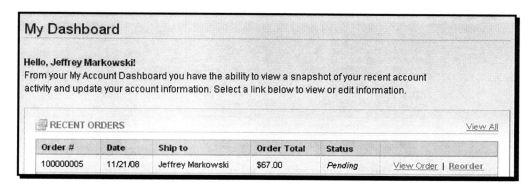

Notice the **Status** of the order.

In the admin interface, you will see this under **Sales | Orders** as shown in the next screenshot:

Notice the **Status** column, second from the right.

If the customer has chosen to pay by check, or money order, and payment for the order has not arrived, the status will be **Pending**. If the customer has chosen to pay using PayPal and the payment has not arrived, the status will be **Pending Paypal**. If the customer has chosen the credit card option and the payment has cleared, the status will be **Processing**. So, in general we can say the following:

- ◆ **Pending**: The order is placed and you're waiting for payment.
- ◆ **Processing**: The order is placed and you have been paid.

At this point, click on the **View** link to open the order. The **Order View** window gives you a snapshot of the order's history and the current status, as shown in the following screenshot:

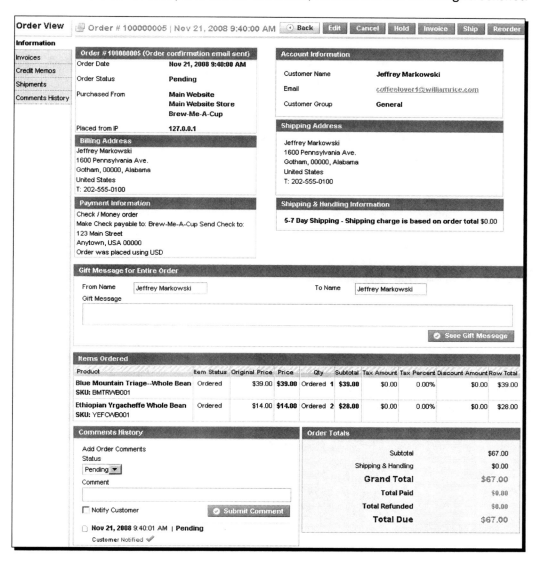

Notice that status of the order is displayed in the lower left corner of the page. If you click on the **Status** drop-down list, you will discover that you cannot change the status of the order:

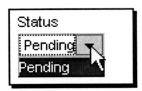

Also, notice the buttons in the upper right corner of the page: **Edit**, **Cancel**, **Hold**, **Invoice**, **Ship**, and **Reorder**. Each of these buttons is an action that you can perform on the order. The status of the order changes as your perform these actions. This is an important concept in Magento's order processing.

 You do not assign a status to an order. The order's status changes automatically as you process the order.

Step 2: You create an invoice

At this point, you could **Edit**, **Cancel**, or place the order on **Hold**. But usually, you will proceed to the **Invoice** step. We will look at **Edit/Cancel/Hold** later. For now, let's continue with the most common process, and create an invoice.

When your customer placed the order, (s)he received a confirmation email from Magento. This email informed the customer that the order was placed. Now, you will create an invoice for the customer. Even if the invoice is never sent to the customer, you should still create it. We will discuss the reason behind this later on.

To create an invoice, click on the **Invoice** button. The **New Invoice** page is displayed as follows:

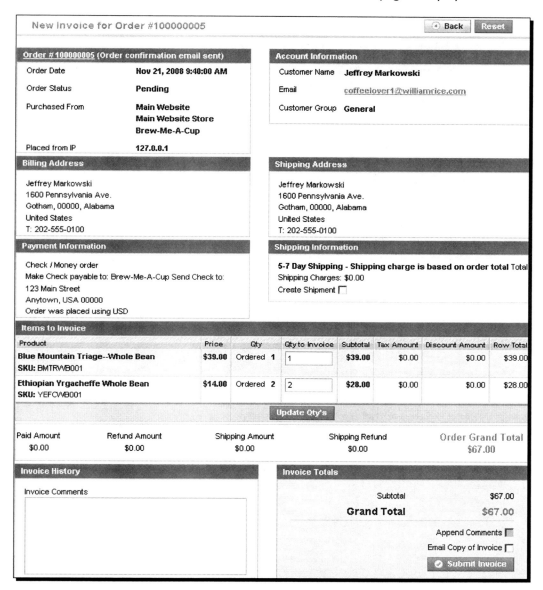

Notice that the **New Invoice** page enables you to do several things as you create the invoice. First, you can email a copy of the invoice to the customer by selecting the checkbox in the lower right corner. This is not required, and it depends upon your business process. As stated before, even if you do not email your customer a copy, you should still generate the invoice.

Second, you can enter comments into the **Invoice Comments** field in the lower left corner. For example, if you've received the check, or money order, you can enter something like "Received check #1000". If the credit card payment has already cleared, you can enter something like "Payment cleared: Authorization number 11111111".

Third, notice that you can change the quantities to invoice. If we can change quantities, we can divide the order in two parts (for example), and make an invoice for each part. This could help if we do not have sufficient stock and would like to send what we have, and send the rest when we receive it.

Clicking on the **Submit Invoice** button creates the invoice. You will be returned to the **Order View** page, where you should see a confirmation message that the invoice was created.

Clicking on the **Invoices** tab displays the list of invoices for this order. You should see the invoice you just created in that list as shown in the next screenshot:

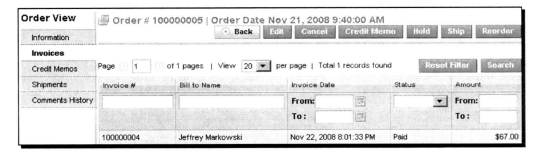

Notice that Magento has given the invoice a status of **Paid**. This is automatic; you cannot do anything about this. As of this writing (Magento version 1.2), when you create an invoice for an order, that invoice's status will be **Paid**. However, the status of the order will be **Processing**. Because of this, you might want to create invoices only after you have received the payment. That way, the invoice's **Paid** status will match your real-world situation. You should put a note in the **Comments** field for your customer that the invoice is paid so that (s)he doesn't think you are sending them a bill.

Step 3: Locate the orders that need to be shipped

Usually, you ship the order after you have received payment. Ideally, you want to be able to quickly locate the orders for which people have paid, so that you can ship their products promptly.

If a customer has paid by credit card or PayPal, and the payment has cleared, the order is quick and easy. In the **Sales | Orders** page, you will see the order status as **Processing**.

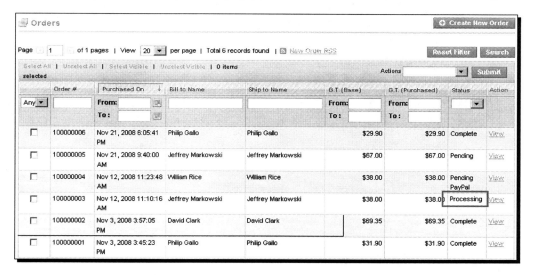

Any order with a status of **Processing** has been paid for, but not yet shipped. Look for these orders, and you will be able to quickly locate the orders that you need to ship.

You can locate the orders with this status by using the **Status** filter to show only the orders with status **Processing**.

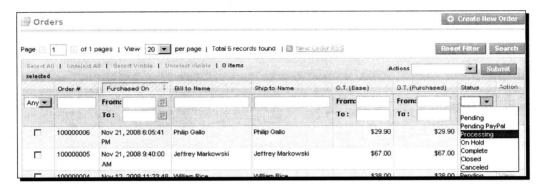

Locating orders that have been paid for by check, or money order, is not as easy. Remember that when a customer places an order and selects **Check** or **Money Order** as the payment method, the order's status is **Pending**. Look at the following screenshot:

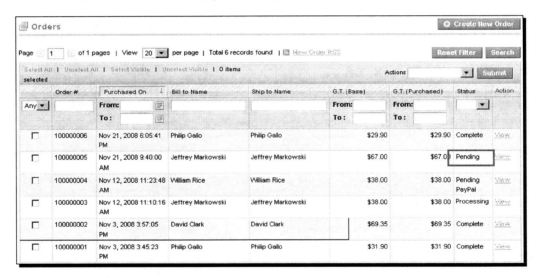

After you generate an invoice, the order's status changes to **Processing**. If you wait to generate the invoice until after receiving payment, then you can just look for all the **Processing** orders and ship them.

However, suppose you send the customer an invoice as soon as you receive their order. This would be a normal business process, which will be as follows:

◆ The customer places an order

◆ The merchant emails the customer with an invoice

◆ The customer prints the invoice and mails a check or money order

◆ The merchant ships the order

The challenge to this workflow is that as soon as you send the customer an invoice, the order's status is advanced to **Processing**. Now you have two kinds of orders whose status is **Processing**: orders for which you have received credit card payment and are ready to ship, and orders for which you are awaiting check/money order payment and are not ready to ship. When you view your list of orders, how can you tell which are paid and ready to ship, and which are not? Using Magento's built-in workflow (as of vesion 1.2), there is no easy way to locate orders that have been invoiced for a check or money order. So, let's look at a workaround.

At any time before an order is completed, you can put an order on hold by clicking on the **Hold** button in upper right corner of the page as shown in the following screenshot:

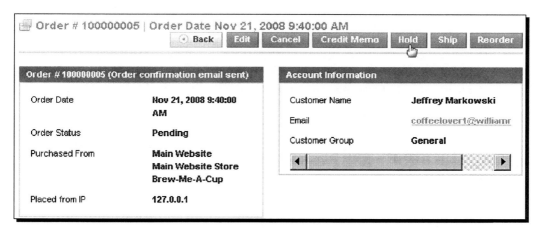

When you receive an order payable by check, or money order, you can use the following workflow:

1. Create and email an invoice to the customer. In the **Notes** field of the invoice, instruct the customer to print this invoice and mail it along with the payment. The order's status is advanced to **Processing**.

2. Immediately, before leaving the invoice page, put the order **On Hold**.

3. When the check or money order arrives (or when it clears—whichever you prefer), take the order off hold. The order's status is back to **Processing**.

4. Now, when you look at the list of orders on the **Sales | Orders** page, you can quickly spot orders with the **Status** of **Processing**, and know that these are the orders you must ship. Look at the following screenshot:

Admittedly, this is not the intent of the **Hold** feature. Normally, a store would put an order **On Hold** for other reasons, such as when an item is on backorder or the customer's payment did not process correctly. However, until Magento adds a way for you to quickly locate orders that you have invoiced but not received payment for, this might give you a workaround.

After identifying the orders that need to be shipped, you are ready to create the shipments.

Step 4: Print orders and pack them

All of this activity needs to result in the actual physical delivery of a product. You must pack and ship these products. If your computer is in the same room as your packing supplies, you can display the paid orders on screen and pack them. If not, you might want to print packing slips and bring them to your warehouse.

For orders that have a status of **Processing**, you can print a packing slip. On the **Sales | Orders** page, click to place a check mark next to the order. Then, from the **Actions** drop-down menu, select **Print Packing slip** and click on the **Submit** button.

Armed with a stack of packing slips and order printouts, you are ready to physically pack your orders. As (or after) you pack them, create shipment notices in Magento. That is our next step.

Step 5: Create a shipment

After locating an order that has been paid for, and packing it, you should open the order in Magento. You will see the familiar **Order View** page. At this page, click on the **Ship** button, as shown in this screenshot:

If the order was on hold, you will need to take it off hold before you can click on the **Ship** button.

Clicking on the **Ship** button creates a new shipment.

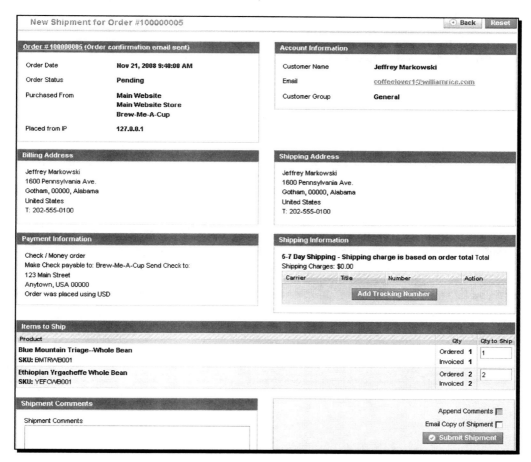

You can add tracking information for this shipment by clicking on the **Add Tracking Number** button.

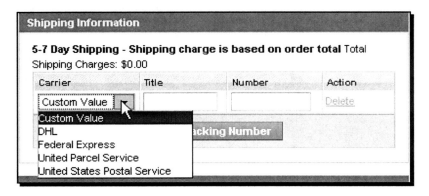

If you choose to send the customer an email from this shipping page, the shipping information that you enter here will be included in that email.

Notice that you can also update the quantities in the shipment under **Qty to Ship**. This enables you to send the items in multiple shipments. You might do this if an item is on a backorder.

 To create additional shipments, you would go back to the **Order View** page and click on the **Ship** button again, generating another new shipment.

You can enter comments about this shipment in the **Shipment Comments** box, in the lower left corner of the page. These comments are visible only to you, unless you select the **Append Comments** checkbox on the lower righthand side of the page. That checkbox will add the comments to the email that is sent to the customer.

When you finish editing the information on this page, click on the **Submit Shipment** button. This records the shipment and changes the order's status to **Completed**, as shown in the following screenshot:

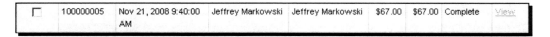

Tips for managing orders

While following an order through the system, you saw some of Magento's advantages and limitations. Because Magento is a very active open source project, its limitations are constantly being replaced by new features.

We want to work within Magento's limitations while taking advantage of its features. Customizing, or hacking, the code is beyond the scope of this book. With that in mind, here are some suggestions for managing orders.

Ship orders paid for with checks/money orders as you process the check

As we saw in the workflow, when an order has been placed and you are awaiting the payment by check, its status will be **Pending**. When you receive the check, you can then generate an invoice. However, the order's status will not change; it remains **Pending**. In that case, both paid and unpaid orders have the status of **Pending**. There is no easy way to locate the orders that have been paid for. For orders that are placed using credit cards and PayPal, this is not a problem. When you receive payment, their order status automatically updates to **Processing**.

Hopefully, Magento will add the ability to manually change the status of an order to **Processing** or **Paid**. Until then, I suggest that you ship orders paid for with checks/money orders as you process them. For each order you should package the order, generate the invoice, and generate the shipment notification—all in one session. The order's status will go straight from **Pending** to **Complete**. This ensures that none of the paid orders get mistaken for unpaid, which could cause you to neglect shipping them.

Be proactive and look for orders that have the status Pending or Pending Paypal for too long

The **Sales | Orders** page enables you to filter the list of orders so that you can show only those with a selected status. It also enables you to sort the list on any of the columns.

Periodically, search for orders whose status is **Pending** or **Pending Paypal**. These orders are unpaid. Then, sort the list by purchase date. If you have orders that have remained unpaid for a long time, you might want to investigate. Did the PayPal payment fail to process? Check your PayPal account. Did you receive a check or money order but you neglected to process it and ship it? Being proactive like this can help you to solve payment glitches before they become problems.

Include a "You're paid up" comment on invoices that you email to your customers

When Magento generates an invoice, it changes the status of that invoice to **Paid**. You can see this status in the list of invoices under **Sales | Invoices**.

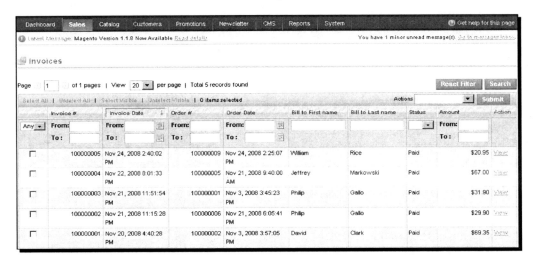

However, when you print the invoice for your customer, it does not explicitly indicate that it has been paid.

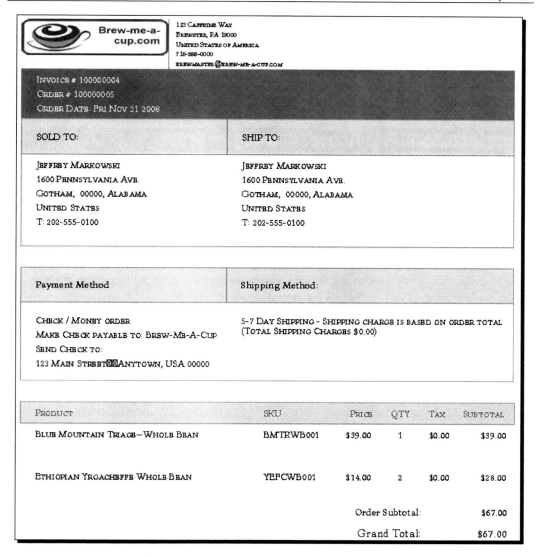

As you saw under the section on generating invoices, you can include a comment in an invoice. If you have received a payment from the customer, add a comment about this to the invoice before sending it to the customer. This will reassure the customer that his or her payment has been received and the order is being processed.

Practicing the complete order process

In the previous chapters we created a customer account on our site, configured at least one payment method (probably check/money order), and configured at least one shipping method (probably flat rate shipping). Now, let's put them all together into one process.

Time for action: Practice processing an order

1. Log in to your store as a fictional customer. Make sure the customer has a valid email address.

2. Place an order. Go through the entire checkout process. If you have configured several payment methods, check out each one.

3. Now, log in to the admin interface.

4. Under **Sales | Orders**, look for the order(s) that you just placed. If you placed an order using the check/money order payment method, it should have the status of **Pending**. If you placed an order with a credit card, it should have the status **Processing**. If you used PayPal, the order should have the status of **Pending Paypal** or **Processing**.

5. For each order, generate an invoice and have Magento email it to the customer. For the check/money order, check whether it advanced to **Processing**.

6. Check whether the customer's email for the invoice(s) is correct.

7. Create shipping notices for each order. Print a packing slip for each order. Check whether their status advanced to **Complete**.

8. Play with as many different scenarios as you can. Test your system and look at the results from both the customer's and admin's view.

Summary

Unlike commercial software, open source software depends upon involvement from the community of users to thrive. Join the Magento community at `www.magentocommerce.com`. Ask and answer questions on the forums. Submit bug reports to the developers. Submit feedback and let developers know what you want from Magento. The more that you take a hand in shaping Magento's future, the more you will get out of it.

A
Abbreviated
Step-by-Step Directions

Categories and Attributes

Creating a Category

1.   Log in to your site's Administrative Panel.

2.   Select **Catalog | Manage Categories**.

Notice that there is already a Category called **Default**.

 Only Categories under **Default** will automatically appear in the Navigation Menu. If a Category is not under **Default**, you will need to create some other way for your customers to get to that Category.

3. If you want this Category to be an Anchor Category, select the **Default** Category. If you want it to be a subcategory, select its Parent Category.

4. Click on **Add Root Category** or **Add Subcategory**. A blank **New Category** window is displayed.

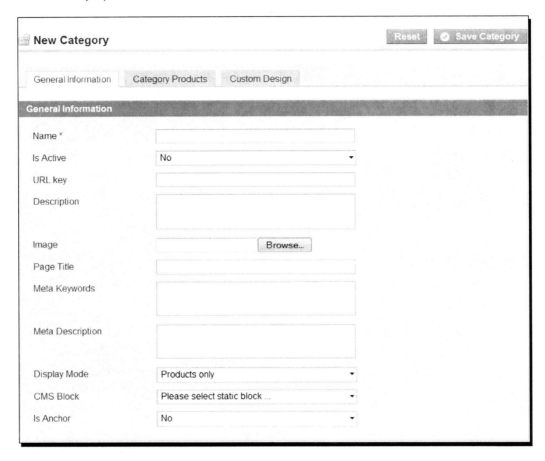

The General Information tab

1. Enter a **Name** for the Category. It will be displayed in your storefront.

2. For the **Is Active** setting, selecting **Yes** makes the Category visible to customers. Selecting **No** will hide this Category and its subcategories in your store.

3. The **URL Key** enables you to enter a search engine friendly path for this Category. If you leave this field blank, Magento will put the name of the Category into this field. Conversely, you can enter the URL path that you want to use for this Category on your site. You cannot enter spaces into this field.

4. The **Description** that you enter here will appear on the Category's landing page.

5. The **Image** that you upload will also appear on the Category's landing page.

6. The **Page Title** appears in the browser's title bar when a customer selects this Category. This is not the same as the **Name**. The **Name** appears in the Navigation Menu at the top of the page, not in the browser's title bar.

7. The **Meta Keywords** and **Meta Description** appear in meta tags, in the page's HTML code. Enter some information about this page, which you think will help search engines to properly categorize this page.

   Use **Meta Keywords** and **Meta Description** as opportunities to optimize the page for search engines.

8. For **Display Mode**, selecting **Products only** will cause the Category's landing page to display a list of products from that Category. Selecting **Static block only** will display only the Static Block of your choice, and no Products. Selecting **Static block and products** will display both.

9. If you chose to show a Static Block, use the **CMS Block** setting to specify which Block to display.

10. If you want this Category to appear in the Navigation Menu, select **Yes** for **Is Anchor**.

11. Click on **Save Category**.

This completes the **General Information** tab for the Category. There are two other tabs, **Category Products** and **Custom Design**. These are optional. You have done what you need to get this Category to work in your store.

Creating an Attribute

1. Log in to your site's Administrative Panel.

2. Select **Catalog | Attributes | Manage Attributes**. A list of all the Attributes gets displayed.

3. Click on **Add New Attribute**. The **New Product Attribute** page is displayed.

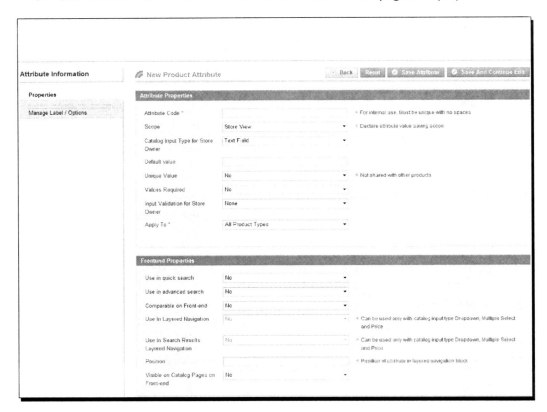

The Properties tab

1. The **Attribute Code** is the name of the Attribute that you will use when managing the Attribute. It must contain only lowercase letters, numbers, and the underscore character. Also, it must begin with a letter.

2. The **Scope** of this Attribute can be set to **Store View**, **Website**, or **Global**. For now, you can leave it set to the default—**Store View**. The other values become useful when you use one Magento installation to create multiple stores, or multiple web sites, both of which are beyond the scope of this book.

3. The field **Catalog Input Type for Store Owner** enables you to select the kind of data that this Attribute will hold.

   If you select **Dropdown** or **Multiple Select** for this field, then under, you will need to enter the list of choices (the list of values) for this field the **Manage Label/ Options** tab.

4. If you select **Yes** for **Unique Value**, then no two products can have the same value for this Attribute.

5. If you select **Yes** for **Values Required**, then you must select, or enter a value for, this Attribute. You will not be able to save a Product with this Attribute if you leave it blank.

6. **Input Validation for Store Owner** causes Magento to check the value entered for an Attribute, and confirm that it is the right kind of data. When entering a value for this Attribute, if you do not enter the kind of data selected, then Magento gives you a warning message.

7. The **Apply To** field determines which Product Types can have this Attribute applied to them. Remember that the three Product Types in Magento are Simple, Grouped, and Configurable.

8. If you select **Yes** for **Use in advanced search**, this attribute will have its own field on the Advanced Search page.

9. If you select **Yes** for **Comparable on Front-end**, this attribute will appear in the Compare Products page.

10. The **Use in Layered Navigation** setting enables your customers to filter Products based on this Attribute. When this is enabled, your customer sees a filter on the left side of the page, where (s)he can select values for this Attribute. Magento will then display only Products that have a value for the Attribute that falls within the range selected by the customer.

    Selecting **No** excludes this Attribute from the Layered Navigation Menu. Selecting **Filterable (with results)** will put the Attribute into the Layered Navigation Menu, but only for those values that show some Products. Selecting **Filterable (no results)** will put the Attribute into the Layered Navigation Menu, and all values will be displayed—even those that don't produce results.

    You can make an attribute filterable only if the **Input Type** is **Dropdown**, **Multiple Select**, or **Price**.

11. If you use this Attribute in the Layered Navigation menu (that is, if you allow your customers to filter by this Attribute), then **Position** determines the position of the attribute in the Layered Navigation. Entering **1** puts this Attribute at the top of the menu.

12. If you select **Yes** for **Visible on Catalog Pages on Front-end**, this Attribute will appear in the **Additional Information** section of each Product that uses the Attribute.

13. Select the **Manage Labels/Options** tab.

14. In the **Admin** field under **Manage Titles**, enter the name that you will use for this Attribute in the administrative interface. In the **Default Store View** field, enter the name for this Attribute that your customers will see in your store.

15. If this Attribute type is **Dropdown** or **Multiple Select**, then the **Manage Options** section will appear.

    In the **Admin** field, enter the name that you will use for this value in the administrative interface. You will see this name when you are creating a Product and assigning a value to the Attribute.

    In the **Default Store View** field enter the value that your customers will see in your store.

    If this Attribute type is not **Dropdown** or **Multiple Select**, then this section will not appear.

16. Click on **Save Attribute**. The Attribute is saved and you are returned to the list of Attributes. You should see the one you just added in the list, and a success message at the top of the page.

    This concludes the process for creating a new Attribute. Repeat this as needed.

Creating an Attribute Set

1. Log in to your site's Administrative Panel.

2. Select **Catalog | Attributes | Manage Attribute Sets**.

    The **Manage Attribute Sets** page is displayed. If this is a new installation, only one Attribute Set will be listed—**Default**.

3. Click on **Add New Set**.

4. Enter a **Name** for this set. You will see the name when you create a Product and need to assign a set to that Product.

5. For **Based On**, select a set that will be the starting point for this set. If this is the first set that you created, then your only choice will be **Default**.

6. Click on **Save Attribute Set**. The **Edit Attribute Set** window is displayed.

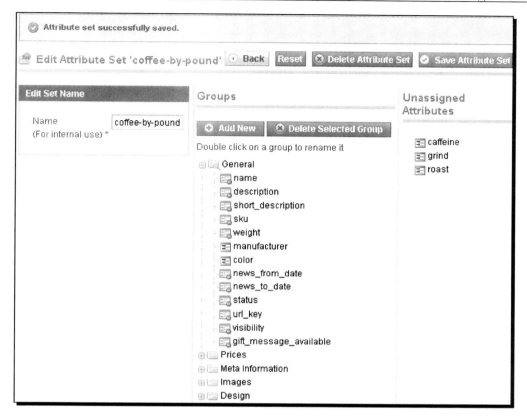

The left column contains the name of this set. The middle column contains all of the Attributes that are a part of this set. Right now, those are the same as for the Default set. The right column contains Attributes that are not a part of this set.

7. To add an Attribute to the set, open a group, and then drag the Attribute from **Unassigned Attributes** into that group.

8. To remove an Attribute from the set, drag it from the group that contains it to the **Unassigned Attributes** column.

9. To move an Attribute from one group to another, just drag and drop the Attribute.

10. To add a new group (and possibly create a new tab on the Product page), click on **Add New**, and enter the name of the new group when prompted.

11. To change the order of the groups, drag and drop them.

    The tabs that these groups create on the Product page display left to right. The topmost group creates the tab on the left, and the bottom group creates the rightmost tab.

12. To delete a group, select it and click on **Delete Selected Group**. You cannot delete a group that has System Attributes in it. When you delete a group, its Attributes become unassigned.

13. When you are finished, click on **Save Attribute Set**.

Taxes

Creating a Customer Tax Class

1. From the Admin Panel, select **Sales | Tax | Customer Tax Classes**.

   The **Customer Tax Classes** page gets displayed. If this is a new installation, only one Class is listed—**Retail Customer**.

2. Click on **Add New**. The **Customer Tax Class Information** page is displayed.

3. Enter a name for the Customer Tax Class.

4. Click on **Save Class**.

Repeat until all of the Customer Tax Classes that you need have been created.

Creating a Product Tax Class

1. From the Admin Panel, select **Sales | Tax | Product Tax Classes**.

   The **Product Tax Classes** page is displayed. If this is a new installation, only two Classes are listed: **Shipping** and **Taxable Goods**.

2. Click on **Add New**.

   The **Product Tax Class Information** page is displayed.

3. Enter a name for the Product Tax Class.

4. Click on **Save Class**.

Repeat until all of the Product Tax Classes that you need have been created.

Creating a Tax Rate

1. From the Admin Panel, select **Sales | Tax | Manage Tax Zones & Rates**.

   The **Manage Tax Rates** page is displayed. If this is a new installation, only two Tax Rates are listed: **US-CA-*-Rate 1** and **US-NY-*-Rate 1**.

2. Click on **Add New Tax Rate**. The **Add New Tax Rate** page is displayed.

3. **Tax Identifier** is the name that you give this Tax Rate. You will see this name when you select this Tax Rate.

4. **Country, State**, and **Zip/Post Code** determine the zone to which this Tax Rate applies. Magento calculates sales tax based upon the billing address, not the shipping address.

   County and **State** are drop-down lists. You must select from the options given to you.

   Zip/Post Code accepts both numbers and letters. You can enter an asterisk in this field and it will be a wildcard. That is, the rate will apply to all zip/post codes in the selected country and state.

   You can enter a zip/post code without entering a country or state. If you do this, you should be sure that the zip/post code is unique in the entire world.

5. Enter the **Rate** and click on **Save Rate**. You are taken back to the **Manage Tax Rates** page. The Tax Rate that you just added should be listed on the page.

Exporting and Importing Tax Rates

1. On the **Manage Tax Rates** page, select **CSV** from the **Export** drop-down menu.

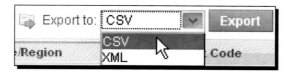

2. Click on **Export**.

3. You will be prompted to save or open the exported file. Choose the option that enables you to open the file in your spreadsheet application.

4. Now that the file is open in your spreadsheet, you can see the column headings in the first row and the Tax Rates in the rows below that.

5. Edit the spreadsheet as needed.

6. Save the spreadsheet as a `.csv`, or text-only, file. Make note of where you save it.

   If Magento gives you an error reading **Invalid file format upload attempt**, your text file is probably saved in Windows, or Macintosh, text-only format. Even though text-only files look the same on Windows, Mac, and UNIX (Linux), they are not. Before Magento can read the file, you need to convert the file to a UNIX format.

   We need to use a text editor designed to work with the Windows/Mac/UNIX formats. On Windows, try the free program TedNPad. On Mac, try TextWrangler.

7. Open the file using a text-editing program. Make sure your spreadsheet application saved the file in the correct format.

8. In your text editor, save the file in UNIX format.

9. In Magento, select **Sales | Tax | Import/Export Tax Rates**.

10. Click on the **Browse...** button and select the file that you created.

11. After selecting the file, click on **Import Tax Rates**.

12. When the file is finished importing, you should see a message stating **Tax rate was successfully imported**.

13. Select **Sales | Tax | Manage Tax Zones & Rates** and check the list of Tax Rates to ensure that yours were imported.

Creating a Tax Rule

1. Go to **Sales | Tax | Manage Tax Rules**.

   The **Manage Tax Rules** page is displayed.

2. Click on **Add New Tax Rule**, and the **New Rule** page is displayed.

   Notice that all of the Customer Tax Classes, Product Tax Classes, and Tax Rates/Zones that you created are displayed here.

3. Enter a **Name** for the Tax Rule.

4. Select one or more **Customer Tax Classes** for the Rule.

5. Select one or more **Product Tax Classes** for the Rule.

6. Select one or more **Tax Rates** for the Rule.

7.   Click on **Save Rule**.

8.   You are returned to the **Manage Tax Rules** page. You should see the Rule that you just added listed there.

Simple Products

Adding a Simple Product

Part 1: Adding the Product and assigning an Attribute Set

1.   Log in to your site's backend, which we call the Administrative Panel.

2.   Select **Catalog | Manage Products**.

   The **Manage Products** page is displayed. As you haven't added any products yet, the list of products is blank.

3.   Click on **Add Product**. The **Product Settings** page is displayed.

4.   Select an **Attribute Set**.

 If you don't know what an Attribute Set is, stop here and read Chapter 3 before proceeding.

5.   Leave **Product Type** set to **Simple Product**. Until you have added several Simple Products, the two choices (**Grouped Product** and **Configurable Product**) don't make much sense.

6.   Click on **Continue**. The **Product Information** page is displayed.

   This page is divided into tabs, which you see listed on the left side. We won't discuss all of the fields on all of the tabs. Instead, we'll cover the fields and tabs that you are most likely to use when you are first creating your store.

   The **General** tab is selected for you. Let's begin there.

Part 2: The General tab

When Magento displays a product in your store, that product appears on its own page. Most of the information that your shoppers see on that page is entered here, on the **General** tab:

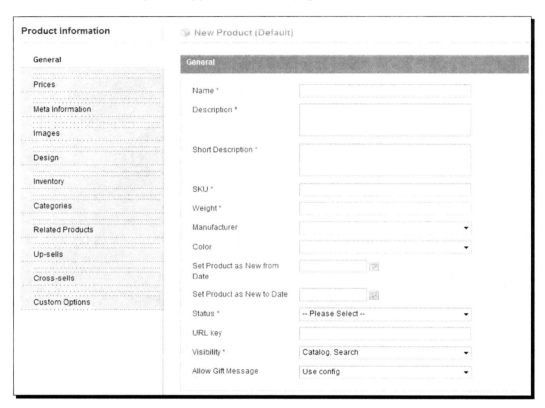

 You must fill in the required fields under the **General** and **Prices** tabs before leaving the **New Product** page. Even if you save your work, the product will not be added to your store if you haven't filled in the required fields.

7. Fill in the **Name** field. Your customers will see the product **Name** at the top of the product's page.

8. Fill in the **Short Description** field. This will display under **Quick Overview** on the Product's page.

9. Fill in the **Description** field. This will display under **Product Description** on the product's page.

10. Fill in the **SKU** field.

11. Fill in the **Weight** field. This should be the product's shipping weight, not the actual weight of the product.

12. If you want Magento to treat this Product as new, then set the dates in the fields for **Set Product as New from/to Date**. If you don't highlight new products in your store, you can safely leave these fields blank.

13. Set the **Status. Enabled** makes this product active and displays it in your store. **Disabled** makes this product inactive and hides it from shoppers.

14. Enter the **URL key** field to create a search engine friendly URL. The URL cannot have spaces or special characters. If you leave this field blank, Magento will generate a search engine friendly URL for you based on the product's **Name**.

15. Set the **Visibility** for this Product. This field determines if the product will not display at all in your site (**Nowhere**), display on the pages of your site (**Catalog**), show up in search results (**Search**), or both (**Catalog, Search**). Note that even if a product's **Status** is set to **Enabled**, your shoppers won't be able to see or find it if you have its **Visibility** set to **Nowhere**.

16. Choose a setting for **Allow Gift Message**. This field determines if customers can add a gift message to this product during checkout. **Yes** and **No** are self-explanatory. **Use config** means that for this product, Magento will use the sitewide setting for gift messages. You will find that setting under **System | Sales | Sales | Gift Messages**.

17. In the upper right corner of the **New Product** page, there are two Save buttons: **Save** will save what you have entered into this tab, and advance you to the next tab. **Save and Continue Edit** will save the information that you entered and keep you on the same tab. Since there is a required field on the next tab, you will want to **Save** this tab and proceed to the **Prices** tab. This is because you must fill in all required fields before the system will allow you to save the product.

Part 3: The Prices tab

18. Enter the normal **Price**.

19. Optionally, enter a **Special price**. If you enter a **Special Price**, the original **Price** will be displayed with a red line through it, and the **Special Price** will be displayed. If you do not enter any dates, the **Special Price** will be in effect until you remove it. If you do enter dates, the **Special Price** is in effect during the dates specified.

20. Enter your **Cost** for the product.

21. The **Tax Class** that you select here determines how the product gets taxed.

[If you don't know what a Tax Class and a Tax Rule are, stop here and read Chapter 4 before proceeding.]

There is more about Tiered Pricing in Chapter 7.

Part 4: Meta Information tab

22. For **Meta Title**, enter the title for this Product page. The title should consist of search terms that customers will use when searching for this kind of product.

23. For **Meta Keywords**, enter keywords that describe this Product. The keywords should be search terms that customers will use when searching for this kind of product.

24. For **Meta Description**, enter a single sentence or phrase that describes the Product. If a potential customer found this Product on a search site like Google or www.ask.com, what description would you like the customer to see? That is what you should enter here.

    Use **Meta Keywords** and **Meta Description** as opportunities to optimize the page for search engines.

Part 5: Images tab

25. On the **Product Information** page, select the **Images** tab.

26. Click on **Browse Files...**. In the dialog box that appears, select one file to upload.

27. Select an image to upload, and then click on the **Open** or **OK** button in the dialog box.

28. If you want the same image to be used for base, small, and thumbnail, you can move to the next step. If you want to use separate images for each of the three images, then click on **Browse Files...** and select more images.

29. After you select all the images that you want for this Product, click on **Upload Files**. The files will be uploaded to the **Images** page.

30. Select the image you want for the base, small, and thumbnail images by clicking the radio buttons.

31. To exclude an image type, click on the radio button in the top row for **No Image**. This means that wherever Magento would have used that image size, Magento will not display an image.

32. Enter a **Label** for each image. This will be used as the "alt text" for that image.

33. Click on **Save And Continue Edit**.

34. The **Design** tab is next on the menu. We will skip that tab because it is beyond the scope of this beginner's guide. Instead, proceed to the **Inventory** tab.

Part 6: Inventory tab

Notice that all of the settings on the **Inventory** tab, except for **Qty** and **Stock Availability**, use the global configuration.

You will find these global inventory settings under **System | Configuration | Catalog | Inventory**.

35. If this is the first Product that you have added, at this point you might want to navigate to **System | Configuration | Catalog | Inventory** and set these global default values. If you open the **System Configuration** page in a new tab, you can keep the Product **Inventory** tab open while you do this.

36. Let's examine each of the fields. Remember that except for **Qty** and **Stock Availability**, each of these fields is found on both the **Product** and **System Configuration** pages. Choose the one you want to edit and navigate to that page. Then, select a setting for each of the following fields:

Field	Appears in Catalog | Manage Products | Product | Inventory	Appears in System | Configuration | Catalog | Inventory	Explanation
Manage Stock	✓	✓	If this is set to **Yes**, then by default Magento will keep a track of the inventory for a Product. If it's set to **No**, Magento will not keep a track of the inventory and all of the other settings that are irrelevant for the Product. The individual setting for the Product overrides the setting for the System.
Qty	✓		This is the quantity that you have in stock.
Set Items' Status to be In Stock When Order is Cancelled		✓	This will "return" items to stock when an order with that item is cancelled. Otherwise, you must manually return the item to stock by adding it to the quantity field.
Decrease Stock When Order is Placed		✓	This global setting makes Magento automatically deduct items from the quantity when those items are ordered.
Backorders	✓	✓	This setting determines if you allow customers to backorder an item that is out of stock.

Field	Appears in Catalog | Manage Products | Product | Inventory	Appears in System | Configuration | Catalog | Inventory	Explanation
Maximum Qty Allowed in Shopping Cart	✓	✓	The maximum quantity allowed in one order.
Qty for Items' Status to become Out of Stock	✓	✓	If the number in stock falls below this threshold, this shows as Out of Stock. If you run both an online and physical store, you might want to keep a few items on the shelf. So, you would set this to some number above zero.
Minimum Qty Allowed in Shopping Cart	✓	✓	The minimum quantity allowed in one order.
Notify for Quantity Below	✓	✓	When the quantity in stock drops below this number, Magento emails the store administrator.
Qty Uses Decimals	✓		This enables shoppers to order a quantity that is something other than a whole number. For example, 1.5 pounds of coffee.
Stock Availability	✓		Magento automatically sets this to **In Stock** or **Out of Stock** based upon the quantity in stock, and the minimum quantity for the item's status to be In Stock. However, you can override this by changing the field yourself. For example, suppose you are out of stock and want to sell a floor model. The floor model is not part of your stock. Therefore, you don't want to add it to your quantity in stock. But because your quantity in stock is zero, Magento won't let you take orders for this Product. You could set Stock Availability to Yes, and that would enable you to take an order for the Product.

Part 7: Categories

37. Under the **Categories** tab, select the Categories in which this Product will reside. Notice that you can select more than one Category.

38. Finally, save the product.

Customizing your store's appearance

Page Cache

To turn the page cache off and on

1. From the admin interface, select **System | Cache Management**.

2. You can select the types of information that Magento will cache. However, when performing basic customization on your site, it is usually easiest to enable and disable all of them at once.

3. From the drop-down menu next to **All Cache**, select **Disable** or **Enable**.

4. Click on the **Save cache settings** button.

Callouts

Replacing the default graphic for a callout

1. Before replacing a graphic for a callout, you should create its replacement. The default callout graphics are 195-pixels wide.

2. Make sure that you have named the new graphic **col_right_callout.jpg** or **col_left_callout.jpg**, whichever one you are replacing.

3. Navigate to the Magento directory **\skin\frontend\default\default\images\media**.

4. Rename the existing **col_right_callout.jpg** or **col_left_callout.jpg** to something else, such as **ORIGINAL_col_right_callout.jpg**. This preserves the original graphic so that you can roll back to the original condition.

5. Copy your new graphic into **\skin\frontend\default\default\images\media** and name it **col_right_callout.jpg** or **col_left_callout.jpg**, whichever one you are replacing.

Replacing the default alt text for a callout

To replace alt text for the right callout

1. Navigate to the Magento directory **\app\design\frontend\default\default\ template\callouts**.

2. Locate the file **right_col.phtml**.

3. Before changing the file, make a duplicate of it. Name it to something like **ORIGINAL_right_col.phtml**.

4. Open the file in a text editor such as WordPad, or in an HTML editor such as DreamWeaver.

5. In the text file, locate the alt text.

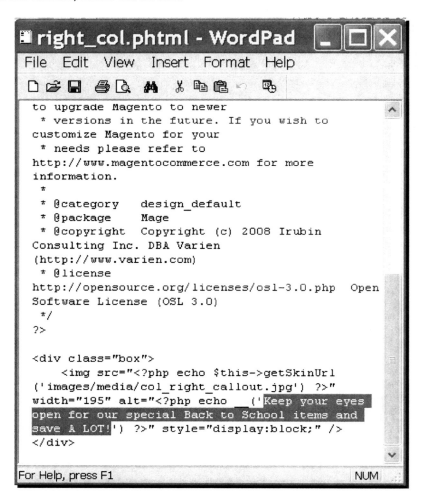

1. Replace the alt text with your own.

```
<div class="box">
    <img src="<?php echo $this->getSkinUrl
('images/media/col_right_callout.jpg') ?>"
width="195" alt="<?php echo    ('We have genuine
Blue Mountain Jamaican Coffee certified by the
Jamaican Coffee Board') ?>"
style="display:block;" />
</div>
```

2. Save the file.

To replace the alt text and link for the left callout

1. Navigate to the Magento directory **\app\design\frontend\default\default\layout**.

2. Locate the file **catalog.xml**.

3. Before changing the file, make a duplicate of it. Name it to something like **ORIGINAL_catalog.xml**.

4. Open the file in a text editor such as WordPad, or in an HTML editor such as DreamWeaver.

5. Locate the default alt text. An easy way to do this is to use the search for **(800) DEMO-NUMBER**.

```
<!--
Default layout, loads most of the pages
-->

    <default>

        <!-- Mage_Catalog -->
        <reference name="top.menu">
            <block type="catalog/navigation" name="catalog.topnav"
template="catalog/navigation/top.phtml"/>
        </reference>
        <reference name="left">
            <block type="core/template"
name="left.permanent.callout" template="callouts/left_col.phtml">
                <action method="setImgSrc"><src>
images/media/col_left_callout.jpg</src></action>
                <action method="setImgAlt" translate="alt"
module="catalog"><alt>Our customer service is available 24/7. Call
us at (800) DEMO-NUMBER.</alt></action>
                <action method="setLinkUrl"><url>checkout/cart</url>
</action>
            </block>
        </reference>
        <reference name="right">
            <block type="core/template" before="cart_sidebar"
name="catalog.compare.sidebar"
template="catalog/product/compare/sidebar.phtml"/>
            <block type="core/template"
name="right.permanent.callout" template="callouts/right_col.phtml"/>
        </reference>
        <reference name="footer_links">
            <action method="addLink" translate="label title"
module="catalog" ifconfig="catalog/seo/site_map"><label>Site Map
</label><url helper="catalog/map/getCategoryUrl" /><title>Site Map
</title></action>
```

6. Replace the alt text with your own.

7. In the next line, notice the link: **checkout/cart**. Replace this with a link of your choice. For example, you could use one of the following links:

To link to this page in your store:	Replace the default link with this text:
Customer Service	customer-service
Contact Us	contacts

8. Save the file.

Disabling the Newsletter or Poll

1. Go to **System | Configuration | Advanced | Advanced**. You should see the **Disable modules output** page.

2. Locate the module labeled **Mage_Newsletter** and/or **Mage_Poll**, and select **Disable**.

3. Click on the **Save Config** button.

Customizing the Welcome Message

1. From the Admin interface, select **System | Configuration | General | Design**.

2. In the **Header** section, enter the **Welcome Text**.

3. Save.

Customizing the HTML Head section

Default Title

If a page in your site does not have a customized title, then it will use the title given here. All of Magento's built-in pages have their own titles, and so this field should not affect your system unless you create custom pages.

Description

This is your store's description. Some search sites will display this in their search results.

Default Keywords

Enter keywords that will help search engines classify your site.

The Header section

The fields in this section are used to customize the logo and welcome message.

Logo Image Src and Alt Text

By default, Magento looks in `\skin\frontend\default\default\images\logo.gif` for the store's logo. The graphic is 157-by-47 pixels in size. The easiest way to customize your store's logo is to make a direction replacement, the same size and file name, and replace the existing one.

The field **Logo Image Alt** holds the alt text for the logo. This will be displayed if the graphic is not.

Welcome Text

Enter your customized welcome message into this field.

The Footer section

On this page, you can change the **Copyright** notice.

There is also a field on the configuration page for **Miscellaneous HTML**. This enables you to add any HTML code immediately below the **Copyright.**

Changing your store's name

1. From the Admin interface, select **System | Manage Stores**.
2. Click the link for **Default Store View**. The **Store View Information** page is displayed.
3. In the **Name** field, enter the name for your store that you want customers to see.
4. Click on **Save Store View**.

Now, whenever Magento displays your store name, it will show the text that you entered.

Customizing the front page

1. Select **CMS | Manage Pages**, and then select **Home page**.
2. In the **Content** field, enter HTML code for your site's front page. You will need to know the basic HTML commands, or use an HTML editor, such as DreamWeaver or Bluefish, to create the HTML code.
3. Change the **Page Title**, which will appear in the title bar of the visitor's browser.
4. Leave the **SEF URL Identifier** field alone.
5. Click on the **Save Page** button.

Advanced Products

To add Related Products to a Product

1. From the Admin interface, select **Catalog | Manage Products**.

2. The list of Products in your store will be displayed.

3. Click anywhere on the Product that you want to edit. Or, you can click on the edit link for that Product.

4. After the Product's page is displayed, select the **Related Products** tab. A search area is displayed. You will use this to search for and select the Related Products.

5. Click on **Reset Filter**. This causes all of the Products in your store to be displayed in the list. Or, enter a search criterion and click on **Search**.

6. To select a Related Product, click to place a check mark in the first column.

7. If this Product has several Related Products, specify the order in which they will appear by entering a number in the Position field, which is in the right-most column.

8. Click on **Save**.

The Related Products that you specified will now be displayed whenever a customer views this Product.

To create a Grouped Product

Part 1: Creating a Blank Grouped Product

1. Make sure that you have created all of the individual Products that will be a part of the Grouped Product.

2. From the Admin interface, select **Catalog | Manage Products**.

3. Click on **Add Product**. The **Product Settings** page is displayed.

4. Select an **Attribute Set**. You do not need to select the same Attribute Set as the individual Products that make up the Grouped Product. You can choose any Attribute Set.

5. For **Product Type**, select **Grouped Product**.

6. Click on **Continue**. The **Product Information** page is displayed.

The procedure for creating a Group Product is almost identical to creating a Simple Product. As you need to create several individual Products before creating a Group Product, these instructions assume that you know how to create a Product. Therefore, they will focus on what is unique about creating a Grouped Product. If you don't understand any part of these instructions, consider reviewing the procedure for creating a Simple Product explained in Chapter 5.

The **General** tab is selected for you. Let's begin there.

Part 2: The General tab

When Magento displays a product in your store, that product appears on its own page. Most of the information that your shoppers see on that page is entered here, on the General tab.

Notice that several fields on this page are marked with red asterisks. These fields are required, and you must fill them in.

You must fill in the required fields under the **General** tab before leaving the page. Even if you save your work, the product will not be added to your store if you haven't filled in the required fields.

7. Enter the **Name**, **Description**, and **Short Description**.

   The way these fields function is similar to the fields for Simple Product. Your customers will see the product **Name** at the top of the product's page. The **Short Description** field appears below that, in the section labeled **Quick Overview**. The **Description** field appears below that.

8. Enter a unique **SKU**.

9. Optionally, enter dates for **Set Product as New from/to Date**.

   A new product can be included in the new product display, RSS feed, and/or an email announcement. Setting dates in the fields for **Set Product as New from/to Date** makes the product new to Magento. If you use any of these features, you will need to fill in these date fields. However, if you don't highlight the new products in your store you can safely leave these fields blank.

   If any of the individual Products that make up the Grouped Product are new, they will also appear as new, in addition to the Grouped Product.

10. Select a **Status** for this Group.

11. Enter a **URL key**.

12. Select the **Visibility** for this Group.

13. Select the setting for **Allow Gift Message**.

14. Save and continue.

Part 3: Meta Information tab

Use **Meta Keywords** and **Meta Description** as opportunities to optimize the page for search engines.

15. For **Meta Title**, enter the title for this Product page. The title should reflect search terms that customers will use when searching for this kind of product.

16. For **Meta Keywords**, enter keywords that describe this Product. The keywords should be the search terms that customers are likely to use when searching for this kind of product.

17. For **Meta Description**, enter a single sentence or phrase that describes the Product.

Part 4: Images tab

18. On the **Product Information** page, select the **Images** tab.

19. Click on **Browse Files...**. In the dialog box that appears, select one file to upload.

20. Select an image to upload, and then click on the **Open** or **OK** button in the dialog box.

21. If you want the same image to be used for base, small, and thumbnail, you can move to the next step. If you want to use separate images for each of the three images, then click on **Browse Files...** and select more images. After you select all the images that you want for this Product, click on **Upload Files**. The files will be uploaded to the **Images** page.

22. Select the image you want for the base, small, and thumbnail images by clicking the radio buttons.

23. To exclude an image type, click on the radio button in the top row for **No Image**. This means that wherever Magento would have used that image size, Magento will not display an image. If you select **No Image** for the thumbnail image, then no image will be added when this is placed in the Shopping Cart.

24. Enter a label for each image. This will be used as the "alt text" for that image.

25. Click on **Save And Continue Edit**.

Part 5: Inventory tab

26. If you want to track the inventory for this Grouped Product, set **Manage Stock** to **Yes**.

27. To make the Grouped Product available to shoppers, select **In Stock** for **Stock Availability**.

Part 6: Categories

28. Under the **Categories** tab, select the Categories in which this Grouped Product will reside. This does not need to be the same category as the individual Products in the Group.

Part 7: Associated Products

Under this tab, you select the Products that are part of this Group.

29. Click on **Reset Filter** to view all products, or enter a search criterion and click on **Search**.

30. To select a Product, click to place a check mark in the first column.

31. Enter a default quantity for the Product. This will pre-fill the quantity field, **Qty**, when the customer selects this Group.

32. Use the **Position** field to determine the order in which the Products is displayed.

33. Click on **Save**.

To create a Configurable Product

Part 1: Designating some Attributes as Configurable

 This section assumes that you know how to create and use Attributes. This was covered in Chapter 3.

1. From the Admin interface, select **Catalog | Attributes | Manage Attributes**. A list of all Attributes in the system is displayed.

2. Click on the Attribute that you want to make configurable. The **Attribute Properties** page is displayed.

3. To make this Attribute configurable, set the **Scope** to **Global**. The Attribute needs to be available everywhere in your site.

4. Set the **Input Type** to **Dropdown**. This creates a drop-down list for the customer.

5. Set **Use To Create Configurable Product** to **Yes**.

6. Click on the **Save** button.

7. Make sure that the Attribute Set that you will use for this Configurable Product contains the configurable Attribute(s) that you just set up.

Part 2: Creating the first Simple Product that will be associated to the Configurable Product

 This section assumes that you know how to create Products. This was covered in Chapter 5.

You must create each Product that will be associated with this Configurable Product. You will create the first Product in the same way as you would any other Simple Product.

After creating the first Simple Product, you will duplicate it and use the duplicate as the starting point for the next Simple Product. This section covers creating the first Simple Product. The next section covers duplicating it and creating the rest of the Simple Products.

8. Immediately after clicking the **Create Product** button, the system displays a dialog box where you select the **Attribute Set** and the **Product Type**.

9. You must select an Attribute Set that has one or more configurable Attributes, such as the one that was set up in the previous section.

   In our demo store, we selected **coffee-by-pound** because it contains the configurable Attribute, **grind**.

10. For **Product Type**, select **Simple Product**. Remember, you are creating one of the Products that will be associated with the Configurable Product, and not creating the Configurable Product itself.

11. After you click on the **Continue** button, the **Product Information** page is displayed. Fill out this page as you would for any Product.

    Pay special attention to the setting for the configurable attribute(s) that you set.

12. Set a unique SKU for each product.

13. Set the **Status** of this Product to **Enabled**, or else it won't be available to your customers.

14. Unlike a normal Simple Product, set the **Visibility** to **Nowhere**. This prevents it from having its own listing in your store.

15. Fill in the rest of the information for this Product, just as you would any other Simple Product. If you need complete instructions, refer to the instructions for creating a Simple Product given in Chapter 5.

16. Save the Product. Now, you are ready to create duplicates of this Product, and use each Duplicate as the starting point for a new Product.

Part 3: Duplicating the first Simple Product and creating the other Products

To begin this part of the procedure, you should keep open the Product that you want to duplicate.

17. Click on **Duplicate**. When the Product is duplicated, you will see a confirmation message at the top of the page.

 You know that you are working with a duplicate Product, and not the original, because the SKU is blank.

18. For the Configurable Attribute, choose a new value.

19. Enter a unique **SKU** for this Product.

20. Set the **Status** to **Enabled**.

21. If needed, edit the **Name** and **Description**.

22. Under **Inventory**, the **Qty** for the new Product is automatically set to zero and the **Stock Availability** is set to **Out of Stock**. You must change these.

23. Look through the tabs for any other information that needs to be changed for this new Product. For example, if you changed the **Name** and **Description**, would you also need to change the **Meta Information**? Does this Product look different enough from the others that you will need to upload new **Images** for the Product?

24. Save this Product.

25. Repeat as needed, until you have created all of the Products that you need for this Configurable Product.

Part 5: Creatinge a blank Configurable Product

26. Make sure that you have created all of the individual Products that will be part of the Configurable Product.

27. From the Admin interface, select **Catalog | Manage Products**.

28. Click on **Add Product**. The **Create Product Settings** page gets displayed.

29. Select an **Attribute Set**. You must select an **Attribute Set** that has one or more configurable Attributes, such as the one that was set up in the previous section.

30. For **Product Type**, select **Configurable Product**.

31. Click on **Continue.** You will see a dialog box asking you to select the Configurable Attributes for this Product.

If there are no Configurable Attributes listed, it means the Attribute Set that you selected for this Product contains no Configurable Attributes. Either go back to **Catalog | Attributes | Manage Attributes** and make at least one Attribute configurable, or start over and select an Attribute Set that has a Configurable Attribute.

32. Select the Attribute(s) that you want to be configurable. This will create a drop-down list for that Attribute, enabling the customer to choose a value for the Product.

33. Click on **Continue**. The **Product Information** page gets displayed.

The procedure for creating a Configurable Product is almost identical to creating a Simple Product. As you need to create several individual Products before creating a Configurable Product, these instructions assume that you know how to create a Product. Therefore, they will focus on what is unique about creating a Configurable Product. If you don't any part of these instructions, consider reviewing the procedure for creating a Simple Product given in Chapter 5..

The **General** tab is selected for you. Let's begin there.

34. Fill in the fields under the **General** tab as you would for any other Product.

35. Remember to enter a unique **SKU**.

36. Remember to set the **Status** to **Enabled**.

37. Unlike the individual Products that make up this Configurable Product, you should set the **Visibility** to **Catalog**, or **Search**, or **Catalog, Search**.

38. Under **Inventory**, the only settings you will see are **Manage Stock** and **Stock Availability**. Set the **Stock Availability** to **In Stock**.

39. Select the **Prices** tab.

40. In the **Price** field, enter the base price for this Product. Later on, you will enter a price modifier for each Associate Product.

41. Look through the tabs for any other information that needs to be changed. For example, will you need a different **Name** and **Description** for the Configurable Product? Will you also need to change the **Meta Information**? Do you want to upload an **Image** that shows several versions of the Product?

42. Click on **Save And Continue Edit**.

Part 6: Associating the Simple Products to the Configurable Product

43. Select the **Associated Products** tab.

44. Click on **Reset Filter** to display all products or, enter search criteria and click on **Search**.

    This causes the Products that use the same Attribute Set to be displayed in the list. The Products that cannot be associated will be shaded, while the ones that can will not be shaded.

45. To select a Product, click to place a check mark in the first column.

46. Click on **Save And Continue Edit.** After saving, Magento takes you to the **General** tab. Return to the **Associated Products** tab.

47. In the **Super product attributes configuration** section, you will see each Configurable Attribute listed.

48. In the **Attribute Name** field, enter the text that you want the customer to see when they choose the setting for this Attribute.

49. In the **Price** field for each setting, enter a price modifier.

50. Finally, save the Product.

Tiered Pricing: Discounts for minimum quantities

1. Select the **Prices** tab.

2. In the Tier Price area, for **Customer Group** select **ALL GROUPS**.

3. In the field **Qty** enter the minimum quantity the customer must buy to get a discount.

4. In the field **Price** enter the special price. This is per unit.

5. Create multiple tiers if necessary.

6. Save.

Customer relationships

Configuring store email addresses

The email addresses that Magento uses to send and receive emails are set up under **System | Configuration | Store Email Addresses**.

Configuring the Contacts Function

1. Make sure that you have an email address that is set up to receive messages from the contact form.

2. From the Admin interface, select **System | Configuration | Contacts**.

3. Expand **Contact Us** and **Email Options** by clicking on them.

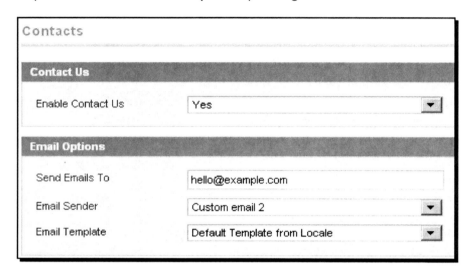

Notice that the **Contact Us** function is enabled by default. Also, notice the fictional email address, which you must change.

4. To display a Contact Us link at the bottom of each page, for **Enable Contact Us** select **Yes**. Selecting **No** will remove the link.

5. In the field **Send Emails To**, enter the email address that you have set up for receiving messages sent by the contact form. Remember, this is the recipient of the form.

6. In the field **Email Sender**, select one of the email addresses that you set up under **Store Email Addresses**.

7. Modifying email templates is beyond the scope of this quick-start guide. Leave the **Email Template** field set to **Default Template from Locale**.

8. Click on the **Save Config** button.

Configuring customer options

Before using customer accounts, you should configure your customer settings. You do this under **System | Configuration | Customer Configuration**. For an explanation of the sections on this page, see Chapter 8.

Accepting payment

Before configuring any of the specific methods for accepting payment (check/money order, PayPal, Authorize.net, Google Checkout, and so on), read and follow the directions in the *Checkout and Sales configuration* section in Chapter 9.

Chapter 9 also contains an explanation of each payment type that is built in Magento. These explanations are meant to help you decide which payment types are best for your store.

The official Magento site also contains add-ons that enable you to accept additional payment types.

Configuring shipping

Before you configure any of the specific methods for shipping (UPS, FedEx, table rates, and so on), read the explanation of each shipping type in Chapter 10. These explanations are meant to help you decide which payment types are best for your store.

Also, you should follow the directions under the section titled *Setting the overall configuration settings that affect shipping*, in Chapter 10.

The official Magento site contains add-ons that enable you to offer additional shipping methods.

Index

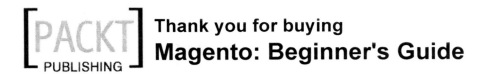

Thank you for buying
Magento: Beginner's Guide

Packt Open Source Project Royalties

When we sell a book written on an Open Source project, we pay a royalty directly to that project. Therefore by purchasing Magento: Beginner's Guide, Packt will have given some of the money received to the Magento Project.

In the long term, we see ourselves and you — customers and readers of our books — as part of the Open Source ecosystem, providing sustainable revenue for the projects we publish on. Our aim at Packt is to establish publishing royalties as an essential part of the service and support a business model that sustains Open Source.

If you're working with an Open Source project that you would like us to publish on, and subsequently pay royalties to, please get in touch with us.

Writing for Packt

We welcome all inquiries from people who are interested in authoring. Book proposals should be sent to author@packtpub.com. If your book idea is still at an early stage and you would like to discuss it first before writing a formal book proposal, contact us; one of our commissioning editors will get in touch with you.

We're not just looking for published authors; if you have strong technical skills but no writing experience, our experienced editors can help you develop a writing career, or simply get some additional reward for your expertise.

About Packt Publishing

Packt, pronounced 'packed', published its first book "Mastering phpMyAdmin for Effective MySQL Management" in April 2004 and subsequently continued to specialize in publishing highly focused books on specific technologies and solutions.

Our books and publications share the experiences of your fellow IT professionals in adapting and customizing today's systems, applications, and frameworks. Our solution-based books give you the knowledge and power to customize the software and technologies you're using to get the job done. Packt books are more specific and less general than the IT books you have seen in the past. Our unique business model allows us to bring you more focused information, giving you more of what you need to know, and less of what you don't.

Packt is a modern, yet unique publishing company, which focuses on producing quality, cutting-edge books for communities of developers, administrators, and newbies alike. For more information, please visit our website: www.PacktPub.com.

Selling Online with Drupal e-Commerce

ISBN: 978-1-847194-06-0   Paperback: 245 pages

Walk through the creation of an online store with Drupal's e-Commerce module

1. Set up a basic Drupal system and plan your shop

2. Set up your shop, and take payments

3. Optimize your site for selling and better reporting

4. Manage and market your site

Zen Cart: E-commerce Application Development

ISBN: 978-1-847191-17-5   Paperback: 300 pages

A step-by-step developer's guide

1. Install, configure, and customize Zen Cart for your customers

2. Enhance and modify Zen Cart

3. Walk through the creation of a fully functional book store

4. Learn advanced features of Zen Cart with practical examples

Please check **www.PacktPub.com** for information on our titles

CPSIA information can be obtained at www.ICGtesting.com
Printed in the USA
244348LV00004B/55-56/P